Papers and reminiscences
appertaining to my first case
with Holmes, March 1881
    John H. Watson. September 1881

Sent to Conan Doyle
        January 1886

Returned from Doyle, May 1886

First appeared under the title
    A Study in Scarlet
in Beeton's Christmas Annual, November 1887
    published by Ward Lock and Co.

A Study in Scarlet

A Study in Scarlet

Based on the Story by
Sir Arthur Conan Doyle

A Sherlock Holmes
Murder Mystery

PEERAGE BOOKS

First published in Great Britain in 1983 by
Webb & Bower (Publishers) Limited in the form of a dossier.

First published in book form in 1985 by
Peerage Books
59 Grosvenor Street
London W1

ISBN 1 85052 045 3

Printed in Hong Kong

THE SAVOY LONDON

SAVOY HOTEL P.O. BOX 189 STRAND LONDON WC2R OEU
Cables SAVOTEL LONDON WC2   Telex RESERVATIONS 24234   MESSAGES 24235
Telephone 01-836 4343

5th January, 1983

The Managing Director,
Webb & Bower (Publishers) Ltd,
9, Colleton Crescent,
Exeter, Devon   EX2 4BY

Dear Sir,

     Would these documents be of any interest to you?
They represent the original papers assembled by Dr Watson
for <u>A Study in Scarlet</u>. It is common knowledge that Watson's
records of his cases with Sherlock Holmes were contained
in a dispatch box, bearing his name, John H. Watson, M.D.,
late Indian Army, painted on the lid. This tin box was kept
in the vaults of the bank of Cox & Co., in Charing Cross,
London. The building unfortunately was destroyed but I can
now reveal that the box has survived.

     Watson once threatened that any attempts to
break into the box would be countered by publication of the
whole story of the politician, the lighthouse and the
trained cormorant. This astonishing tale is now in my
possession and will undoubtedly cause an uproar when it is
made public. I have also the original papers on many other
unpublished cases, as well as those on the sixty published ones.

     How I came by the box is a singular tale in itself;
it was a fortunate but entirely accidental discovery - a
fine example of serendipity - not entirely unconnected
with a wartime liaison mission and the Savoy Hotel, just
down the road from Charing Cross. The box was produced
out of London's rubble like buried treasure, but I will tell
you all about that if we meet and I will explain to you then
why I have not been able until now to make known the contents
of the box.

       Yours faithfully,

Simon Goodenough

10th. January, 1886

My Dear Conan Doyle,

    When we met at that pleasant luncheon in the Café Royal,
you were generous enough to express considerable interest in
the papers I had collected concerning the first case I shared
with Sherlock Holmes. I believe you said that you were out of
the country at the time the events took place, but you were
evidently acquainted with the circumstances.

    You will appreciate that my notes were not at first
intended for publication but I had some amusement in collecting
the evidence and compiling a little folder of reminiscences
which I had printed in facsimile form and passed round to a
number of interested friends. Since then, Holmes himself has
shown some curiosity about what I have been doing and, you
will observe, has added some of his own notes. I must confess
that this was done rather behind my back and perhaps you will
not think that all his observations have a place in the story.

    I am delighted you agree that there could well be
something worthy of a wider audience in these reminiscences
and I shall be most obliged if you will arrange any small
editing that is required and approach a publisher. I thought
some title like A Tangled Skein would suit - Holmes has made
a note somewhere about studying the scarlet thread of murder
that runs through the story; it was certainly a very tangled
thread. By the way, I have just realized that today is the
fifth anniversary of my meeting with Holmes!

    Yours most sincerely,

    John . H. Watson

STATEMENT of the Services of *John. H. Watson*

of the *Army Medical Department* Regiment of — with a Record of such

Particulars as may be useful in case of his death.

Where born *Nr Winchester, Hampshire*   Date of birth *18ᵗʰ September 1852*

Age on entering the Service *27 Years*   Whether a Cadet at the Royal Military College *No*

RANK.	Regiment or Half Pay.	Date of Appointment.	FULL PAY. Whether obtained with or without Purchase; and, if by Exchange, whether with or without paying the difference.	HALF PAY. Whether obtained by Reduction, or by the Purchase of a Half-Pay Commission; whether in consequence of his being from ill health incapable of Service, or under what other circumstances; if by Exchange, whether with or without receiving the difference.
Previous Services (if any) in the Ranks .... }	*None*	‿	‿	‿
Lieutenant............... *Surgeon*	*Army Medical Department*	*12ᵗʰ March 1880*	*Without Purchase*	
Captain				
Major				

PERIODS OF EMPLOYMENT.

Station.	At Home		Abroad.	
	From	To	From	To
United Kingdom Netley Medical Course —	*15ᵗʰ September 1878 (with interruptions)*	*11ᵗʰ March 1880*	—	
India and Afghanistan —			*12ᵗʰ March 1880*	*26ᵗʰ November 1880*
United Kingdom Medical Furlough	*26ᵗʰ November 1880*			

Campaign.	Battle, Siege, Action.	Date.	Regimental or Staff Situation held on the occasion.	Name of Officer in Chief Command.	In what or whose Despatches mentioned, and terms used as regards the Officer, with date of London Gazette or General Order.
Afghanistan	Maiwand	27th July 1880	Surgeon	General Burrows	General Orders Bombay Castle September 1880

HAS FILLED THE FOLLOWING SITUATIONS ON THE STAFF.

Appointment.	Station.	Period.		Total Period in Years and Months.
		From	To	
Surgeon - with Rank of Lieutenant Attached: 1 Fifth Northumberland Fusiliers 2 Royal Berkshires 66th Foot	Bombay / Kandahar	26th April 1880	30th October 1880	6 months

WOUNDS.

Action in which received.	Date.	What Grant of Pay has been received.	Rate of Pension, Date, and whether Permanent or Temporary.
Maiwand. Shoulder wound and suspected leg injury Enteric Fever.	27th July 1880	Full pay of Lieutenant	Full pay for 9 months from 1st December 1880

TITLES, HONORARY DISTINCTIONS, AND MEDALS.

Distinctions.	Date of receiving such, and for what Service.	Whether promoted for Service in the Field.	Whether granted any Pension for distinguished Service, and if so, the amount.
None	—	—	—

negotiations with the Albanian League have arrived at Scutari. Mustapha Pasha, the President of the Commission, has made frequent endeavours, but without success, to obtain the consent of the Committee of the League to the cession to Montenegro of the portion of Albanian territory which has been assigned to the Principality.

CYPRUS.

LARNACA, JULY 27.

Major-General Sir Robert Biddulph, the High Commissioner of Cyprus, accompanied by his family and part of his staff, left here to-day for the hill district of Troados.

RUSSIA.

ST. PETERSBURG, JULY 28.

The great annual fair at Nijni Novgorod opened yesterday.

The new clipper Opritchnik will be launched to-morrow from the Baltic works. She measures 204ft. between the perpendiculars and 32f. in breadth, and will be armed by four 6-inch guns.

FRANCE.

PARIS, JULY 28.

General Faure, Minister of War, M. Varroy, Minister of Public Works, and M. Constans, Minister of the Interior, will accompany President Grévy on his visit to Cherbourg. It is stated that M. Freycinet, Minister for Foreign Affairs, will remain in Paris, being detained here by the negotiations connected with the Eastern Question.

THE VATICAN.

ROME, JULY 28.

The Apostolic Delegate at Buenos Ayres has sent a despatch to the Pope upon the result of his mediation for putting a stop to the recent civil war between the Nationalists and Provincials, and His Holiness, in reply, has expressed his satisfaction at the success attending the Delegate's efforts.

The Vatican has decided to open direct relations with the Hellenic Government, through the intermediary of Monsignor Marango, with the object of protecting the spiritual interests of the Catholic population in the Turkish districts to be ceded to Greece.

The Roman Catholic inhabitants of the Rhenish Provinces, after a meeting at Cologne, at which a resolution was adopted asserting the supremacy of Church over State, forwarded an address to the Pope on the subject; but the Vatican, considering it inexpedient at the present juncture to send any reply of an explanatory character, has resolved merely to acknowledge the receipt of the address, without entering into the details of the question.

VICTORIA.

MELBOURNE, JULY 27.

The new Victorian Parliament has been opened by the Governor, the Marquis of Normanby, who, in his speech, after alluding to the deficit in the revenue for the year, expressed a hope that Parliament would pass a satisfactory measure for the reform of the Constitution. His Excellency further announced the introduction of Bills dealing with the questions of the land department, the extension of railways, and the construction of irrigation works.

Mr. Berry subsequently moved a vote of want of confidence in the Cabinet of Mr. Service, which was passed by 48 votes to 35.

CUBA.

HALIFAX, JULY 27.

The captain of a vessel from Turk's Island reports that the governor of the island has refused the demand of a Spanish cruiser for the surrender of a Cuban insurgent leader and 40 of his followers, who had been landed on the island as fugitives by a mail steamer from Hayti.

THE UNITED STATES.

NEW YORK, JULY 27.

A site has been selected in the Central Park for the obelisk which was recently brought to America from Egypt.

Three men have been suffocated by black damp in a mine near Pottsville, Pennsylvania.

JULY 28.

There is little change in Dr. Tanner's condition this morning, his pulse being at 84; temperature, 98; respiration, 14; and weight, 130lb.

AFGHANISTAN.

Lord Hartington announced in the House of Commons yesterday the receipt of the following telegram:—

From Governor of Bombay, dated July 28, 1880.

"Primrose telegraphs to-day from Candahar:—'Terrible disaster. General Burrows's force annihilated. We are going into citadel. General Phayre telegraphed to collect what forces he can, and march on Candahar. Posts are being concentrated at Chuman.' I have telegraphed Simla we can send another brigade if necessary."

[This announcement appeared in our Third Edition of yesterday.]

We have received the following telegrams from the India Office for publication:—

"From Viceroy, July 28, 1880.

"General Burrows has been seriously defeated by Ayoob Khan. Primrose has vacated cantonments at Candahar and retired to citadel. We are pushing forward reinforcements already on their way, as quickly as possible, and sending large additional reinforcements from India. It may be necessary to anticipate despatch of troops from England intended for this season's reliefs."

"From Governor of Bombay, July 28.

"Clear the line. Horse Artillery, E-B Battery, 3d Bombay Cavalry, 3d Scinde Horse two squadrons, 2d Company Sappers, 66th Queen's six companies, 1st and 30th Native Infantry. Nothing more known; telegraph interrupted."

(REUTER'S TELEGRAM.)

SIMLA, JULY 28.

General Burrows has been severely defeated by Ayoob Khan. He sustained great loss, and his forces were dispersed and compelled to fly, being pursued by the enemy for three miles. They are now straggling back to Candahar in driblets. Two guns were lost.

Orders have been given to General Phayre to concentrate his force and move forward to Candahar immediately to support General Primrose. His line of communication with the rear will be strengthened by the Bombay and Bengal troops, who are under orders to march without delay.

Before the United Service Institution, on June 16, Major-General Sir Michael A. Biddulph gave an interesting sketch of his experiences of the march of the columns commanded by him "from the Indus to the Helmund and back, 1878-9":—

"Candahar stands on the western side of the plain which was originally a barren skirt of the mountain. Exactly opposite the city, and two miles to the westward, there is a wide break in the dividing range through which the road to Herat leads, and by which are conducted the many canals and watercourses taken from the Argandab to supply the town and fertilize its environs. The energy and skill displayed in these extensive waterworks cannot be too high extolled. Brought from a point many miles distant in the Argandab Valley, the chief canal with its offshoots conducts a vast body of water, which is dispersed along the contours of the declining plain in innumerable channels, spreading a rich fertility for many miles in a fanlike form to the south-east of the gap. Villages cluster around the city on three sides. Cornfields, orchards, gardens, and vineyards are seen in luxurious succession, presenting a veritable oasis within the girdle of rugged hills and desert wastes all round. And if we turn to the aspect of the country beyond the gap we see in the Argandab Valley, along the canals and the river-banks a fair and beautiful landscape of village and cultivated ground stretching for many miles in each direction. If we could cast our eyes still further we should see in the vales of the Tarnak and Arghesan districts scarcely less fertile.

"This productive character of the immediate neighbourhood of Candahar and its commanding position within

Yesterday Mr. Justice Lush and Mr. Justice ceeded with the hearing of the petition of Mr against the return of Mr. T. Garfit, the Conser member for Boston. The principal witness Caister, who admitted having given bribes to voters on behalf of Messrs. Garfit and Rowley Q.C., submitted on the part of Mr. Garfit that way connected with these transactions. E however, adduced to show that addresses jointly by Messrs. Garfit and Rowley and the also circulated bearing the words, "Vote f Rowley." In other ways also the joint can shown. Mr. Day, Q.C., asked that Mr. Gar sworn to disprove certain allegations made personally. Mr. Garfit was then sworn and s had no knowledge whatever of any corrupt pr behalf and that he never provided any money purposes, except that stated in his election acc Day, Q.C., said it was impossible for him general evidence which had been given. Mr. concurred and declared that Mr. Garfit w elected; the costs to follow the event.

The petition presented against the return of the Liberal sitting member, was then proc Three or four persons admitted having receiv excess of railway fares for which ostensib provide. The Court adjourned until to-day.

LIVERPOOL.—Mr. Rathbone has definitive allow himself to be put in nomination for the at Liverpool, vacated by Lord Ramsay. It that Mr. Rathbone's refusal to enter on an was emphatic at the outset, but the managemen the Nine Hundred persuaded him to withhold sion till it was seen whether the Conservative his unopposed return. The unanimous sele Claud Hamilton by the Constitutional A proved the hopelessness of winning Conservat for Mr. Rathbone, and that gentleman's refu now made known. The names of Mr. Pli member for Derby, Mr. Henry Yates Thomp a candidate for South Lancashire in 1865, a gentlemen are mentioned in connexion wit ture. It is understood that three names will to the Nine Hundred for selection to-day. T of Lord Claud Hamilton has been very favou by the public on the Conservative side. I expected in Liverpool to-day, and will be the A. B. Forwood, the Priory, Gateacre, but th public meeting of the Conservatives till holiday, so that the season's recreation may rupted. The address of Lord Claud Hamilto night, refers to a number of public questions himself a Conservative, an attached member blished Church, and a warm supporter of relig He says that events have justified the app which the present Government's advent i viewed, the system condemned seven years euting and pestering every interest having be with renewed force and vitality. The Gove cipitate policy in the East has created the p hensions in Europe, and promoted a spirit of rebellion which may produce serious conse lordship promises to support the Governmen of policy calculated to maintain the dignity abroad and the fulfilment of treaty obligatio dition of Ireland, he says, is still a matter anxiety; and he continues, "An intimate with the country convinces me that rest and agitation, security of life and property, an of capital afford the true and only means o removing the chronic disaffection which Her Majesty's Government have recommen ment measures of a totally different charac principles utterly subversive of the foundatio and contravening that freedom and validi which are the great sources of national p earnest desire is to promote the happiness my fellow-countrymen in Ireland, and I ready to give my best attention to legisla the attainment of that end." Referring to t tion, he says that he will gladly support any is equitable in its application to employer the same time affords adequate security to their lives in their daily occupation He p attention to temperance legislation and to shipping matters, and concludes by expressi he will have opportunities in a few days of fully into questions of public interest.

SCARBOROUGH.—The nomination of c place at Scarborough yesterday. The Rig George Dodson (Liberal) was proposed Horatio D'Arley, and seconded by Mr. Geor Arthur Duncombe (Conservative) was

the new shares, and now stands at

ctors of the National Bank of New Zea- ed) report that the year's profits for the on the 31st of March last were £83,332, £1,721 brought forward. Expenses took this, and rebate on bills not due £7,292, et balance of £22,529. Out of this an vidend at the rate of 6 per cent. has en paid, absorbing £10,500, and it is make a similar distribution now. This £1,529 to be carried forward. The et shows a liability of £1,576,814 on current account, and a note circulation 6. It is announced that Mr. Charles M.P., has resumed the chairmanship of

esired to state that the appellants in the The London Guarantee and Accident Limited) v. Fearnley," which was de- e House of Lords on Tuesday, are not rantee Society," of 19, Birchin-lane, no such proviso in its policies as that the subject of the litigation.

ctors of the New Quebrada Company nnounce the issue of £100,000, in six ebentures "secured by a charge upon ny's entire undertaking, including their Venezuela, comprising 275,000 acres of nd, and upon the annual *minimum* re- 16,000." The money is wanted to dis- existing debenture and floating debt of ny. The price of issue is £85 per £100 At present the debenture debt is 8 per cent., and £20,000 at 10 per cent. received the following notices :—

aring Brothers and Co. notify the payment the 1st proximo, of the interest and also a the Koursk-Kiew Railroad shares.

. Corbett, writing from 85, Gracechurch- states that the business hitherto carried on style of "Thomas Corbett," Australian and d merchant, ceased on the 30th of June last, and e be carried on by Messrs. Laughland. Mackay,

STATE OF TRADE.

AND, JULY 27.—The pig iron trade has been steady, and the fluctuations in price have not rked. At the beginning of the present week 3, and 43s. 6d. No. 4 forge was the quotation, per ton. less has been taken, mostly by mid- nasters are not very ready to sell in what they ikely to prove a rising market. They quote 45s. No. 3. Certain of the merchants who are e desirous of bearing the market have been ell No. 3 over the whole year at 44s. Manufac- egitimate consumers have lately bought pretty g iron to cover contracts, as they have been w work, and seem to be inclined to regard the favourably. There is more inquiry for manu- on, and prices have been stiffer. The general ip plates is about £6 15s., but manufacturers ll off for work ask £7 ; bars are £5 17s. 6d. to £6 to £6 2s. 6d. less the usual commission. her more inquiry for foundry material. Ship- manufactured iron from the Tees have been there has been an average delivery of pig iron, the Continent. Coke is firmer, sellers asking y, but no change can be reported as a rule in ing coals.

28TH.—Butter—Firsts, 116s. ; seconds, 112s. ; ; fourths, 95s. ; fifths, 78s. Superfine, 125s.; 20s. ; mild, 116s. Firkins in market, 1,553.

OOL, 28TH.—The demand for cotton on the dily maintained, and has resulted in a fair busi- prices for all descriptions. The sales are 8,000 rising 6,830 American, 40 Brazil, 500 Egyptian, , and 600 Surat, and including 1,000 on specu- for expert. Futures opened at a decline of sponse to the fall at New York yesterday, but red the decline, and close firmly at last night's e New York market is telegraphed firm at about ance. Business in the sugar market con- moderate, but there is no change in prices. clude 100 tons Taal at 15s. 9d. ex quay ; 180 e concrete at 21s. 3d. ; and 300 bags Egyptian 7s. 9d. to 28s. per cwt. Rice is quiet ; nothing leum quiet. Tallow very steady at late prices.

GHAM, 28TH.—There have not been many ctions in the lace trade since our last report, s is rather quiet. Cotton fancy goods, however,

STOCKS and RAILWAY and OTHER SHARES.

PRINTING-HOUSE-SQUARE,
Wednesday Evening.

The next monthly settlement in Consols is fixed for the 4th of August, and the fortnightly settlement in Railway Stocks, Foreign Bonds, &c., begins on August 11 and ends on August 13.

The following are the 4 30 p.m. prices in Consols, Indian and Colonial Funds, in the leading English Railways and Foreign Stocks, and in such other securities as are subject to frequent fluctuations :—

In the market for ENGLISH GOVERNMENT SECURITIES, Consols closed at 97¾ 97⅞ for money and 97¾ 97⅞ for the account, and New Three per Cents. at 97⅝ 97¾. India Four per Cent. Stock FELL ¼ to 104 104½, and the Four per Cent. Bonds 2s. to 43s. 48s. prem. Board of Works Stock FELL ½ to 104 104½; and the Scrip ¾ to 4 4½ prem.

In COLONIAL BONDS, New Zealand (Four per Cent.) ROSE ¼ to 87¾ 88¼.

In INDIAN RAILWAY STOCKS, Madras (Five per Cent.) RECEDED ½ to 121½ 122½, and Scinde, Punjab, and Delhi ½ to 121½ 122½.

BRITISH RAILWAYS.—A RISE of ½ in North Staffordshire to 87 87½. A FALL of 1¼ in South-Eastern (Deferred) to 132¼ 132¾ ; 1 each in London, Chatham, and Dover (Ordinary) to 31⅜ 31⅝, ditto (Four-and-a-Half per Cent. Preference) to 102½ 103, and North British to 76⅞ 77⅛ ; ¾ each in London and Brighton (Deferred) to 160¼ 161, Metropolitan District to 82½ 83, North-Eastern to 165⅜ 165⅝, and Manchester, Sheffield, and Lincolnshire (Deferred) to 62⅞ 63⅛ ; ⅝ in ditto (Ordinary) to 94 94½ ; ½ each in Caledonian to 110¾ 111, Great Northern (A) to 122½ 123, London and Brighton (Ordinary) to 150 152, and Metropolitan to 122½ 123 ; and ⅜ each in London and North-Western to 157⅜ 157⅝ and Midland to 137⅜ 137⅝.

UNITED STATES, COLONIAL, AND FOREIGN RAILWAYS.—(4 15 p.m. Prices.)—A FALL of ½ in Atlantic and Great Western (2d Mortgage) to 28¼ 28¾ ; ¼ in ditto (1st Mortgage) to 67¾ 68¼ ; ⅛ in Grand Trunk (Ordinary) to 20⅞ 21⅛ ; and 1-16 in Great Western of Canada to 13¾ 14. (3 p.m. Official Prices.)—A RISE of 2 each in New York Central and Hudson River (Dollar Bonds) to 130 135 and Philadelphia and Reading (Improvement Mortgage) to 87 89 ; 1 each in ditto (General Consolidated) to 106 108, Grand Trunk (Perpetual Debentures) to 106½ 107½, Central Uruguay of Montevideo (Six per Cent. Debentures) to 104 106, Baltimore and Potomac (Main Line) to 109 111, ditto (Tunnel) to 108 110, and Eastern of Massachusetts to 102 104; ½ in Mexican (Perpetual Debentures) to 111 113 ; and ¼ each in ditto (Ordinary) to 4¾ 5¼, ditto (1st Preference) to 21½ 22, ditto (2d ditto) to 13½ 14, and Lima to 4¾ 5¼. A FALL of ¼ in Namur and Liége to 11½ 12.

FOREIGN RAILWAY OBLIGATIONS.—A FALL of 1 each in Charkof-Azof to 90 92, Charkow-Krementschug to 90 92, North-Western of Montevideo to 22 24, and Provincial Orel Vitebsk to 89 91 ; and ⅛ each in South Austrian to 10½ 10⅝, ditto (1871) to 10⅜ 10⅝, and South Italian to 10⅜ 10⅝.

TELEGRAPHS.—A FALL of ¼ in Anglo-American (Ordinary) to 62¼ 62¾ ; and ⅛ each in West Coast of America to 2¼ 2½, West India and Panama to 1½ 1¾, and ditto (1st Preference) to 7⅛ 7⅜.

FOREIGN GOVERNMENT SECURITIES.—An ADVANCE of ½ each in Argentine (1868) to 86 87 and ditto (1871) to 83 84 ; and ⅛ in United States (Funded) to 105⅜ 105⅝. A FALL of 1 each in Austrian Gold to 73½ 74½, Turkish (1854) to 83 85, and ditto (1871) to 67½ 68 ; ⅞ in Russian (1873) to 87⅛ 87⅜ ; ¾ each in ditto (1862) to 86¾ 87¼, ditto (1870) to 89 89½, ditto (1871) to 88¼ 88¾, ditto (1872) to 87¾ 88¼, and ditto (1875) to 79½ 80½ ; ⅝ in Egyptian (Preference) to 86⅞ 87⅛ ; ½ each in ditto (Unified) to 59⅞ 60⅛, ditto (Khedive, New) to 69½ 69¾, ditto (State Domains) to 90¾ 91¼, Hungarian (1871) to 85½ 86, ditto (1873) to 85 85½, Turkish (1858) to 15 16, and ditto (B and C) to 16 17 ; ¼ each in Peruvian (1870) to 17 17½, and ditto (1872) to 15⅛ 15⅜ ; and ⅛ each in French Rentes (Five per Cent.) to 117¼ 117¾, Hungarian Gold to 90 90½, Italian to 81½ 82, Turkish (General Debt) to 9¼ 9⅜, ditto (1873) to 9¼ 9½, and United States (Four per Cent.) to 112¼ 112½.

PARIS BOURSE.—To-day's 3 15 p.m. prices are compared with those at 3 12 p.m. yesterday :—Rentes, Three per Cent., for money, 84f. 40c.—a rise of 5c. ; ditto, for the account, 84f. 50c.—a rise of 20c. : ditto, New, 86f. 5c.—a rise of 15c.; ditto, Five per Cent., for money, 119f. ; ditto, for the account, 119f. 5c.—a rise of 5c.; Italian, Five per Cent., 83f.; Lombards, 177f. 50c.; Austrian Railways, 597f. 50c.; Suez Canal, 1,151f. 25c.—a rise of 1f. 25c.; Ottoman Bank, 485f.—a fall of 1f. 25c.; Turkish, Five per Cent., 9f. 55c.; Austrian Gold, 74f. 93c.—a rise of 18c.; Spanish, Three per Cent., 18f. 87½c.; Egyptian, Preference, Five per Cent., 437f. 50c.; ditto, Unified, Six per Cent., 305f. 62c.—a rise of 1f. 25c.

The following are other changes recorded in the Official List up to 3 p.m. :—

In BANKS, an ADVANCE of ¼ in Queensland National to 8 8½. A DECLINE of ½ in London and County (New) to 33 34 ; and ⅛ in Commercial of Alexandria to 2⅞ 3⅛.

BRITISH POSSESSIONS.

Atlantic and St. Lawrence Sh., 6 p.c., acc., 124½ 3½ 4¾
Bombay, Baroda, and Central India, 126¼
Canada, Cent. of, 5 p.c., 1st Mort. Bonds, 104¼
Do., acc., 104⅜
East Indian, 4½ p.c., Annuity A, acc., 22⅞
Do., Def. Ann. Capital, gua. 4 p.c., 125 ¼
Do., acc., 125⅝
†Gd. Trunk of Canada, Con. Stk., 21⅛ 1
†Do., acc., 21 ¼ ⅝
Do., Equip. Mort. Bonds, acc., 103¾
Do., 1st Pref. Stock, 91¾
Do., acc., 91⅞ ½ ⅝ ¾ ½ ⅝
†Do., 2d Pref. Stock, 77⅝
†Do., acc., 78 7⅞ 8⅛ 7¾ 8¼‡ 7⅝ 8 7⅞
†Gd. Trunk of Canada, 3d Pref. Stock, 40
†Do., acc., 40⅝ ¼ ⅛ ⅛ ⅛ ¼ 40 39¾ 40⅛
Do., 5 per cent. Perp. Deben. Stk., 107¼
Do., acc., 107⅛ ¼ ⅜ ¼ ⅛ 7
Gt. Indian Penin., g. 5 p.c., 127 6⅞
Do., acc., 126½
Gt. West. of Canada Sh., acc., 14
Do., 5 p.c. Pref., 97½
Hamilton and N.-West., 1st Mt., 6 p.c., 99⅛
Do., acc., 99½ ¼
International Bridge, 6 p.c. Mort. Bonds, 2d Series, acc., 102⅝
Madras, gua. 5 p.c., acc., 122 1¾
Madras. Irrig. and Canal, gua. 5 p.c., acc., 103½
Scinde, Punjab, and Delhi, gua. 5 p.c., 121¾
Do., acc., 122 ¼

FOREIGN RAILWAYS.

Central Argentine (l.), gua. 7 p.c., acc., 16¾ ½
Cent. Uruguay of Montevideo (l.), perm. 6 p.c. deb.stk., acc., 104¾
Dutch Rhenish, acc., 29⅝
Gt. Western of Brazil (l.), gua. 7 p.c., acc., 22⅜
Lemberg-Czern-Jassy (l.), g. 5 p.c., 1 and 2 issue, acc., 14¼
Nizam's State Railway, 6 p.c. gua., acc., 109
Mexican (l.), acc., 6 9-16 ⅝ ¾ ⅛ ¾ ⅝
Do., 1st Pref., 8 p.c., acc., 21⅝ ⅝ ¾
Do., 2d Pref., 6 p.c., acc., 13¾ ⅝ ¾ ⅝
Do., 6 p.c. Perpet. Deb. Stock, acc., 111½ 12 ¾ ⅛
San Paulo (Brazilian) (l.), g. 7 p.c., 34½ ⅜

FOREIGN RAILWAY OBLIGATIONS.

Central Argentine, 6 p.c., 109
Dutch-Indian, 4½ p.c., 80½
Prov. Orel Vitebsk, gua. by Russia, acc., 90
South Austrian, 10¼ ⅝
Do., 1871 (Series X), 10½
Do., acc., 10⅝ ¾
Varna, 3 p.c., 5
Do., 6 p.c., 4⅛

AMERICAN BONDS AND SHARES.

CURRENCY BONDS AND SHARES.

†Atlantic & Gt. West., 1st Mt. Trst. Certs., 68
†Do., acc., 68⅛ ⅜ 8 7⅞ 8¼
†Do., 2d Mort. Trst. Certs., 28⅜
†Do., acc., 28½ 9 8¾
†Do., 3d Mrt. Trst. Certs., 13⅝ ¾
†Do., acc., 14 13⅞ ¾
Baltimore & Potomac (Mn. Line), 1st Mort., 110
Central of New Jersey, Con. Mort. Assenting, acc., 108¼
Central Pacific of California, Land Grant Bonds, acc., 110⅝
Chicago, Milwauk, & St. Paul, 1st Mort., S.-W. Div., acc., 108¾
Detroit, Grnd. Haven & Milwauk. Con. Mort., 106
Illinois Cent., $100 Shs., acc., 110½
New York Central and Hudson River $100 Shares, div. pay. in Lon. at 4s. 1½d., acc., 135⅞
New York, Lake Erie, & Western, $100 Shares, acc., 45¼ ⅝
Do., 6 p.c. Pref., $100 Shs., acc., 73½
Do., 2d Con. Mort. Bnds., acc., 93½
Pennsylvania, $50 Shares, acc., 58⅛ 8 ⅛
Philadelphia and Reading, $50 Shares, 9¾
Do., acc., 10⅛ 10 9⅞
St. Louis Bridge, 1st Mort. Gold Bonds, acc., 109¼
South Pacific Rail. of California, 1st Mort. Bonds, acc., 102½

STERLING BONDS AND SHARES.

Baltimore and Ohio, 1895, 6 p.c., acc., 117½ ⅞
Do., 1910, acc., 118
Do., 1877, 5 p.c., 105¼
Eastern Rl. of Massachusetts, 102½
Illinois Central Sink. Fund, 105½
New York Central and Hudson River Mort. Bonds, acc., 119½
Pennsylvania, Gen. Mort., 118½ ⅞
Pennsylvania, Con. Sinking Fund Mort., 114¼ ¾
Philadel. and Erie, 1st Mort. (g. by Penn. Rail.), 102¼
Philadel. and Reading, Improvement Mort., 88⅛
Do., acc., 88½ ¼ 7¾ ⅞
Do., Gen. Mort., 60
Do., acc., 60⅜ ¼ 59¾ 60

BANKS.

Agra (l.), acc., 11
Anglo-Egyptian Bank (l.), acc., 25 4¾ 5
Bank of Africa (l.), acc., 14½
Bank of Australasia, acc., 79½
Bank of Brit. Columbia, acc., 17½
Bank of New Zealand, acc., 22½ ⅛ ¼
Bank of Roumania, 11½ ⅝
English Bank of Rio de Janeiro (l.), acc., 11⅜
English, Scottish, and Australian Chartered, acc., 24¾
Imperial (l.), acc., 16
Imperial Ottoman, 9⅝
Do., acc., 9 5-16 ½
International Bank of London (l.), acc., 15¼
London & County (l.), acc., 67¾
Do., New Scrip, iss. at £10 pm., £2 10s. paid, 34½ 3½
Do., acc., 34 3⅞ ¾ ½
London and Provincial (l.), 11⅝
London & River Plate (l.), acc., 11⅝
London and South-Western (l.), acc., 21
London & Westminster (l.), New, 26⅛ ½
Lon. Chartered of Australia, acc., 24¾
†Mercantile Bk. of Riv. Plate (l.), acc., 2⅞
Merchant (l.), acc., 32¾
National Provincial of England (l.), 44⅞
Do., 1880, acc., 18½
Oriental Bank Corporation, acc., 18⅞ ½ ⅞
Queensland National (l.), acc., 8¼
Standard of British South Africa (l.), 54
Do., acc., 54¼
Union of Australia (l.), 63⅛
Do., acc., 62¾ 3

TELEGRAPHS.

Anglo-American (l.), acc., 62⅝ ¾
Do., Preferred, acc., 92¾ ¼
Do., Deferred, 35¾
Do., acc., 35¾
Direct United States Cable (l.), 1877, acc., 12⅛ 12 ⅛ 12 ⅛
Eastern (l.), 9 7-16
Do., acc., 9⅜
Do., 6 p.c. Pref., 12½
Do., acc., 12⅝
Eastern Exten., Australasian, and China (l.), 9½
Eastern and S. African (l.), 5 p.c. Mort. Deb., 102¼
Globe Telegraph and Trust (lim.), 6 p.c. Pref., acc., 12⅝
Great Northern, acc., 9⅝
London Plat.-Brazilian (l.), acc., 5
Submarine, Scrip, acc., 2⅜
West Coast of America (l.), 2⅝
Do., acc., 2 7-16
West India & Panama (l.), acc., 1½
†Western and Brazilian (l.), acc., 6 9-16 ⅝

INSURANCE.

Commercial Union, acc., 19⅞
Fire Insurance Association (l.), acc., 2 9-16
Nth. British & Mer., acc., 52¼‡ ⅛
Thames & Mersey Mar., acc., 11⅛
Universal Marine, (l.), 10⅞

GAS.

British, acc., 36
Gas Light & Coke, A, Ord., 188½
Do., acc., 188¾ 7¾‡ 9
Do., 4½ p. c., acc., 108½
Imp. Continental, acc., 188¾ ½ 9
Montevideo, acc., 16¼ ⅜ ⅛ ⅝
Para (l.), acc., 6½

WATERWORKS.

Grand Junction, max. 10 p.c., 109
Odessa (l.), B, acc., 2⅛ ¼

BONDS, LOANS, AND TRUSTS.

American Investment Trust (l.), Preferred, acc., 106½
Do., Deferred, acc., 95¼
City of Montreal, 5 p. c. Sterling, acc., 105
City of Wellington (N.Z.), 6 p. c. Cons. Deb. 1907, acc., 108¾
Egyptian, 7 p. c. Viceroy Mort. Loan, 80½‡
Do., 9 p. c., gua. by Egyptian
Foreign and Colonial Gov. Trust (l.), Pref., acc., 109½
Governments Stock Investment (l.), acc., 15½
Lyttelton (N. Z.) Harbour Board, 6 p. c., 1929, acc., 107⅜
Railway Share Trust (l.), A, acc., 8¾‡
Russian 5½ p. c. Land Mortgage, 2d Series, acc., 86¾

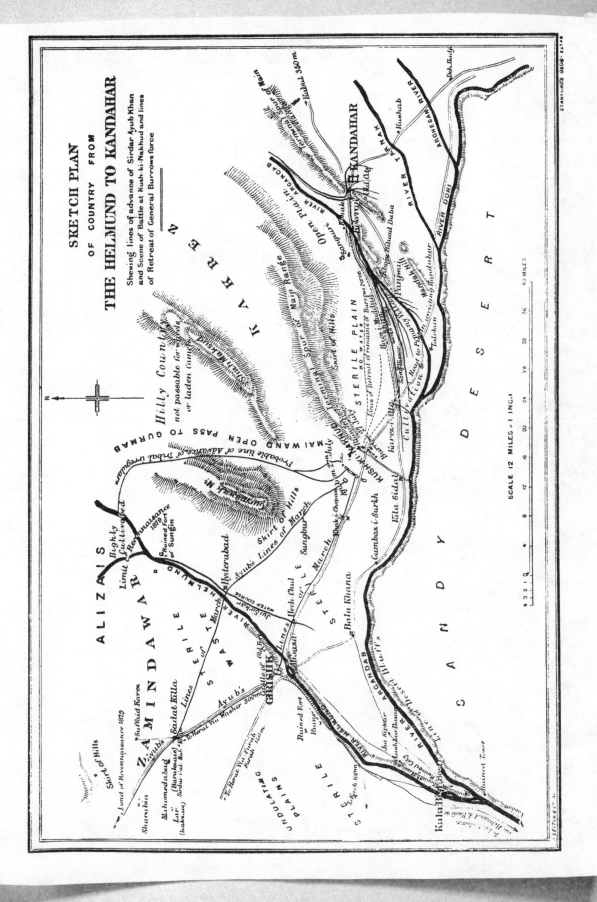

SKETCH PLAN

OF COUNTRY FROM

THE HELMUND TO KANDAHAR

Shewing lines of advance of Sirdar Ayub Khan
and Scene of Battle at Kush-ki-Nakhud and lines
of Retreat of General Burrows force

SCALE 12 MILES = 1 INC.¹

STANFORD'S GEOG. ESTAB.

intermittent fever after one injection. When they were killed they presented very marked enlargement of the spleen, which contained large masses of dark brown pigment. The spleen and the lymphatic glands contained very small, bright corpuscles, which developed, after twenty-four hours in a suitable medium, into threads filled with spores. Formation of pus or any other changes due to inflammatory or septic processes of the different organs were entirely absent.

In further experiments, cultivated bacilli taken from urine, or the isinglass mixture, furnished the material for the injections, and always with the same positive results. The soil, taken from different places in Rome itself and the Agro Romano, proved, in nearly every instance, efficacious also. But the injection with water standing over the marshy ground remained without effect.

Of course it was necessary also to try soil free from malaria. Professor Klebs took infusions of the soil of the garden in the pathological laboratory at Prague. The results remained in this case somewhat doubtful, because the animals became ill, but not in the same way as before, so that it seemed that a mere septic injection had taken place. Two rabbits became ill and died with symptoms of septic poisoning spontaneously at Rome, so that it was possible to compare the two processes directly; and the pathological conditions found in the dead bodies proved different in these latter cases, because pus was found, pigment was totally absent, and the spleen, although enlarged, had lost its firmness.

Afterwards Dr. Marchiafava at Rome was able to demonstrate spores and bacilli in the spleen, the marrow, and the blood of three persons who had died of pernicious fever, showing the same characters as those observed by Klebs and Tommasi-Crudeli.

In summarising the results of their investigations, the authors consider the following facts as proved:—(1) That it is possible to reproduce malarial infection in every form in rabbits in which it is known in men; (2) that the malaria produced artificially in animals is generated by organisms existing in the malarial soil at the time when the outbreak of the fever has not yet taken place. We see, therefore, that those experiments, although small in number, have led to very important results. It is to be hoped that they may become the starting-point for further investigations in the same direction. As the authors themselves allow, there are still many points which require further elucidation. But it is encouraging to see how, by a comparatively small number of careful experiments, good results can be arrived at, when a strictly logical and methodical course of investigation has been pursued.

AUTOPSIES IN LESIONS OF THE STOMACH.—In a paper read at the Société de Biologie, Dr. Dumaschino observed that as in France autopsies are not made until twenty-four hours after death, changes may be produced in the stomach (from cadaveric imbibition, *ramollissement*, post-mortem chemical action, etc.), imputable to the action of the gastric juice and decomposition of alimentary substances. These changes may be prevented by the injection into the stomach of alcohol at 80° by means of an œsophageal tube one or two hours after death. He exhibited the stomach of a child, two months old, into which such injection had been made. The mucous membrane was found in a perfect state of preservation, all the component structures being easily distinguishable by the microscope.—*Gaz. des Hop.*, January 8.

SULPHURIC ACID AS A PROPHYLACTIC IN CHOLERA.—Dr. MacCormac, Consulting Physician to the Belfast Royal Hospital, has written two letters to the Secretary of State for India, urging the prophylactic use of dilute sulphuric acid during cholera epidemics. Everyone living within the affected area is to have ten drops in a teaspoonful of peppermint-water once or even twice daily. The remedy is, at all events, very economical, for a pennyworth of the acid in England will render 1200 persons "approximatively safe for one day and night." Dr. MacCormac relies apparently upon a solitary experience of its effects which he gained during the occurrence of cholera at Belfast in 1854; and it seems strange that the remedy should find support in what cannot but be considered a very remote and limited practice; but measures are to be at once taken to bring the "specific" under the notice of medical officers, both civil and military in India.—*Indian Medical Gazette*, December.

ORIGINAL COMMUNICATIONS.

PRACTICAL NOTES ON
THE ORDINARY DISEASES OF INDIA,
ESPECIALLY THOSE PREVALENT IN BENGAL.
By Dr. CHEVERS.

(*Continued from page 365 of last volume.*)

NOTE ON TRUE ENTERIC FEVER IN INDIA.

MY knowledge of the recent progress of this disease in the East has received several important accessions since the publication of my last chapter on the subject in September.

In his presidential address at the Epidemiological Society,(a) Sir Joseph Fayrer mentions that the Sanitary Commissioner's Report of 1877 says that, out of 233 cases of typhoid, 92, or 39 per cent., proved fatal; the admission-rate being 4·1 per 1000 of strength. It moreover appears that 2·45 per cent. occurred at or under 24 years of age; 1·55 at 25 to 29; 0·99 at 30 to 34; and few or none above that age; showing that the disease tells most severely on the younger men—in this respect resembling typhoid in England. Again, Dr. Bryden, in his report of the Statistical History of the European Army in India up to 1876 (published in 1878), says: "It has no geography; and it is a matter of popular observation that no regiment or battery escapes enteric fever *in the first year*, whatever cantonment of India may be selected." "Out of seventy-three bodies of men, two regiments and seven batteries only returned no case of enteric fever in the first year." And he gives the following analysis of 368 deaths that occurred between 1823 and 1876:—

Ages.			Total Deaths.
24 and under	.	.	255
25 to 29	.	.	90
30 to 34	.	.	17
35 to 39	.	.	4
40 and upwards	.	.	2

Seventy-five of these deaths occurred within three years after landing in India, and 94 per cent. of the total were among men under thirty years of age. In a memorandum which Sir Joseph Fayrer had lately received, Dr. Bryden wrote that, out of 132 deaths from enteric fever in 1878, 90 occurred in men who had been under twenty-two months in India.

Dr. Furnell's valuable paper on True Enteric Fever in Madras(b) appears to have been written before he read my second chapter on this disease. Far from doubting the existence of this malady in India, I there give my own experience of it during my last ten years' service, in addition to the experience of Twining, Ewart, Edward Goodeve, and others. Dr. Furnell's observation corroborates my own, to the effect that, hitherto, it has occurred very distinctly but not very frequently among the civil population of India. He says: "We have quite, in Madras (I mean the town proper), made up our minds not only to its existence, but to its being, occasionally, anything but rare. During the cold season of 1878-79 it was very common, and I had, in my wards, several times as many as half a dozen cases together. I was sceptical at one time of its common occurrence, but last year quite removed my doubts." Dr. Furnell gives one typical case in a Hindoo. He says that, previous to the occurrence of this case, he had not seen any cases in natives, or he had overlooked them. In like manner Dr. Porter, of the Madras Medical Department, states(c) that "reported cases of undoubted typhoid among natives are rare."

I have lately had a very interesting conversation with a practitioner of great experience in Ceylon, who informs me that True Enteric Fever is of such frequent occurrence in the *pettah* (native town) of Columbo, that he has, of late, found it very difficult to convince his younger medical brethren that some of their cases are examples of Paludal Remittent, and must be treated as such.

In discussing a case which they freely admit presents, in all other respects, the typical characteristics of True Enteric Fever, Dr. Gordon and other Indian observers appear to be met by the objection—Can this case be distinctly traced to

(a) Delivered November 5, 1879.
(b) *Medical Times and Gazette*, page 631, vol. ii. 1879.
(c) *Indian Medical Gazette*, April 1, 1878.

the direct effects of filth-poisoning? If not, we cannot accept it as an example of True Enteric Fever. Upon this point, I can only say that, in all probability, there is no country in the world in which impregnation of the soil with cesspool filth is so general as it is nearly throughout the Plains of India. I lately met with a correspondence which I had many years ago with the late Colonel James, then Executive Engineer of Berhampore, at the end of which he tells me that my prescription for the *cure* of the great tank attached to the barracks at that station had been successful. Marvellous to relate, the barrack drains were led into this otherwise noble sheet of water, out of which the soldiers used to drink! A brother-officer told me that he saw the water black, with bubbles of noxious gas floating upon its surface. It is not surprising that these most costly barracks were, after many years of terrible mortality, declared to be untenable by European troops. In writing upon the sanitary prospects of Calcutta, I once had occasion to inquire: Given a loaf of bread that has been thoroughly saturated with sewer-filth—how is it to be purified? and what means, within reach of our science, are to cleanse the loose soil of this city, which has thus soddened for two hundred years? The rural inhabitants of Bengal frequently change the locality of their dwellings. I have travelled over nearly the whole of the plain country of the Delta, and I believe that there are very few eligible localities which have not, at some time or other, been occupied by huts. Dr. William Palmer tells me that he has been particularly struck with this point, in its bearing upon the causation of Enteric Fever, when engaged in the examination of potable waters in his capacity of Chemical Examiner to Government. He very rarely found a Bengal water free of traces of contamination by animal filth. The Calcutta Midaun, a large grassy plain between the City and Fort William, is generally supposed to have been originally rice-fields. An apparently unexceptionable site for a new tank having been selected there, in what was imagined to be virgin soil, Dr. Palmer found the condition of the water to be such as to lead to the discovery that a village had formerly occupied that spot. I think that it may be fairly inquired—Is there any bazaar in India, accessible to European soldiers, in which a thirsty man may not obtain a draught of filth-impregnated water? Nay, more, is there any such place, out of the Presidency-towns which have good water supplies, in which there is the slightest hope of obtaining a draught of perfectly unexceptionable water?

Facts have recently been afforded by Surgeon-Major A. Clark,(d) and by Surgeon-Major Black,(e) showing that, although the recent experience of ten years in Natal led Dr. Brinsley Nicholson to conclude that True Typhoid had not occurred in that country, this disease prevailed rather extensively among our European Troops during the Zulu Campaign. We have thus placed before us the suggestive fact that very young soldiers, when conveyed by the most rapid means of transit, suffer, soon after arriving in India or in South Africa, from True Enteric Fever, a disease which appears to be rare among the native and civil European inhabitants of those countries. Consequently it is needful (1st), as Sir Joseph Fayrer points out, that, in selecting troops for service there, the men's age should be well considered; and (2nd) that a company or two of soldiers should be sent to India in slow-sailing vessels by the old route round the Cape, and that it should be most carefully observed whether True Enteric Fever occurs among them either during the voyage out or within the first six months of their residence in India.

(*To be continued.*)

A BILL has been introduced into the American Senate, the object of which is to compel railroad and steamboat companies, carrying passengers from one State to another, to make use of the best possible contrivances for the security of these passengers. The Bill proposes the appointment of five commissioners, to be nominated by the President and confirmed by the Senate, whose duty it shall be to decide what contrivances shall be used, and if they be inventions, to fix the rate of compensation to which the owners of the inventions shall be entitled for the use.

d. As cited in Sir Joseph Fayrer's recent Presidential Address to the Epidemiological Society.
(e) *Medical Times and Gazette*, vol. ii. 1879, page 554.

HÆMORRHAGE WITH A CONTRACTED UTERUS.

By A. H. F. CAMERON, L.R.C.P. Edin., M.R.C.S. Eng.

IT is generally assumed that the amount of contraction of the uterus after parturition is a fair gauge of the probability or not of hæmorrhage, and when good contraction is present the practitioner generally feels assured that there is little danger, and may thus be lulled into a false security, and perhaps be tempted to leave his patient at the most critical moment. But it is unquestionable that cases occur in which alarming hæmorrhage takes place while the uterus is well contracted. On the other hand, an enlargement of the uterus soon after delivery, *if unaccompanied by pain*, is, in my experience, unimportant. These views, though contrary to the current opinions among obstetricians, have been forced upon me by repeated experience, and I have been much interested by finding the same views enforced and ably illustrated in a very learned paper by Dr. Gooch, published in the *Medico-Chirurgical Transactions* for 1823. In this he says: "Experience has taught me that there are two circumstances in which a hæmorrhage sufficient to produce alarming symptoms may occur, though the uterus feels contracted in the ordinary degree."

The two classes of cases thus noted by Dr. Gooch are— 1st. Cases in which, from some peculiarity of constitution, the patient is singularly prone to syncope. 2nd. Cases in which the force of the circulation is *extraordinarily* great, so as to overcome the *ordinary* closure of the orifices by the uterine contraction. I forbear to quote further, but must refer my readers to the paper itself.

The following case presents some features differing from those related by Dr. Gooch. The patient, a lady about forty years of age, has had several children, and her labours have been usually attended by a considerable amount of hæmorrhage. She is of a rheumatic constitution, and has suffered from endocarditis, and has now a soft systolic bruit, probably due to mitral incompetence. Her labours have been generally tedious, and, thinking that the exhaustion consequent on this tediousness might probably be the cause of the hæmorrhage, I determined to expedite delivery by the early application of the forceps, but the last two labours have been so quick that this has been impracticable; nevertheless, hæmorrhage has occurred to an alarming extent about three-quarters of an hour after delivery.

On the last occasion, as the placenta did not readily come away, I introduced my hand and removed it, thinking thus to excite reaction of the uterus and prevent hæmorrhage, but without effect. At the usual time, though the organ was well contracted, the alarming symptoms occurred; they were controlled, however, and the patient progressed favourably. For some days there was, however, a fœtid discharge, as had been the case after the previous confinement, and about the seventh day a rigor occurred, followed by a temperature of 103°; the next morning the temperature sank to the normal point, with a considerable purulent discharge, clearly indicating that something had been retained in the uterus. The placenta had been carefully examined and found entire; no part of that, therefore, could have been the cause of the symptoms, but I observed that the uterine surface had a roughened appearance, though there was no apparent adhesion. May it not have been the case that some portions of the placental structure, sufficient to prevent the closure of the orifices of the uterine vessels, may have remained behind? This would be probably sufficient to set up hæmorrhage at that period, when, I think, some relaxation of the uterus usually takes place, viz., about three-quarters of an hour after delivery.

This, too, may account for the fœtid discharge by the natural decomposition of the small portions of placental structure referred to. It must be remembered, too, that the patient had a weak and ineffective heart, and my experience leads me to infer that any weakness or diseased condition of the heart has a decided tendency to the production of post-partum hæmorrhage, and may perhaps be the explanation of many of those cases classified by Dr. Gooch under his first head. I have consulted Dr. Angus Macdonald's work on the bearings of heart disease upon parturition, but do not find that he acknowledges hæmorrhage as being referable to this condition. He says (page 204), "at the labour the chief

Saturday. 1st May   1880

Spring in England but not here in India. Arrived in Bombay to find my regiment, the Fifth Northumberland Fusiliers, had already advanced through the passes into Afghanistan to meet the threat of major hostilities in the war. Ordered to make immediate arrangements to sail to Karachi and thence to Candahar. The thought of another long boat trip is depressing but I shall be glad to get out of the busy stench of the city.

Monday. 28th June

With my regiment now for several weeks and busy making preparations. Everyone tight with anticipation. Great confidence but no knowledge of our plans until today. I have been newly attached to the Royal Berkshires, 66th Foot, under the command of Brigadier-General Burrows. In less than a week we are to move forward with a large British force against Ayub Khan's Ghazis and Pathans. We shall see what they are really worth!

Friday. 9th July

We are South of a small village called Maiwand.

having been forced to retreat when Ayub Khan
out-flanked our advance, which began five days ago.
He had clear intelligence of our plans. The men are
put out but not lacking in spirit.

Sunday. 26th July.
    News that the enemy are close and the
possibility of action soon. Everyone keyed to a
high pitch of excitement. Now is our chance to
come to grips with the Heathen.
            My next entry will be news of
victory. I have no doubt!

Saturday, 20th November   1880

Less than a week's sailing away from Portsmouth and
home. I have even now barely recovered from the
fever. For the first half of the voyage from Bombay, I
felt completely wretched. I never thought it would be so
long before I wrote in my journal again, but my condition
has been such that I almost forgot about it. After
our fatal engagement with the enemy on the day
after my last entry, I should have fallen into the
hands of the murderous Ghazis had it not been for
good old Murray, my orderly, who threw me
across a pack-horse, and succeeded in bringing me
safely through. With a group of other wounded, I
escaped internment with the rest of the force in
Candahar, and reached the base hospital at Peshawar
across the border. The ordeal of this journey did not
help the shoulder wound I had received from a
Jezail bullet, which had shattered the bone and grazed
the subclavian artery. It took me some while to
recover from this and my other wounds, which
at first appeared less serious, and I had only just
begun to bask a little on the verandah, when I was
struck down by enteric fever, that curse of our Indian

possessions. It seemed as if it was for months that my life was despaired of, though it was barely a matter of weeks, but it won me this medical furlough back to England.

Sunday 19th December

Well ensconced in the Strand Hotel and quite lively back in London again. On my arrival at Portsmouth on November 26th, went immediately to Netley to visit old comrades at the Army Medical College and then on to visit relatives in Hampshire before travelling to London. The old haunts of my student days and my period as a house surgeon at Bart's, are very much the same, though I am not entirely strong enough to enjoy them to the full. Acquired a rather fine bull-pup for exercise but some difficulty in concealing it from the hotel management I find it splendid for making acquaintances in the park, particularly with the young ladies, who regard his boisterous vigour with pretty trepidation.

Strand Hotel,
The Strand,
London.

8th. March, 1881

Dear Dr. Watson

        We must with regret draw your attention
to the unhealthy appearance of your account, which has not
improved since we brought its ailing condition to your
notice this time last week. We are already charging you an
exceptionally favourable rate for bed and breakfast and we
can only suggest, with great respect, that further to
reduce your expenses, you forego the breakfast or vacate the
bed, or do both. We have also reason to believe that you
are concealing a dog on the premises.

        I remain yours respectfully,

                                        A. J. Smythen

                                Manager.

What does he expect
Income =   11/6 per day
Hotel = 7/6 "   "
Evening Meal = 3/6 "   "
              11/-

Cheapest decent
dinner for two costs
£1.

= 6d per day for tobacco,
wine and whiskey   Impossible!!

Monday, 10th. January, 1881

The New Year not much more than a week old and I have already made a remarkable acquaintance. Heaven knows what will come of it but let no one say that John Watson was slow to seize on fresh experience.

The events of this day made me determined to revive an earlier habit, to keep, beside the brief entries in my occasional journal, more extensive notes, written at leisure, on matters of peculiar interest. If only the disciplines of my student years had reasserted themselves sooner. The scarce leaves of my journal kept safe throughout my extraordinary adventures in Afghanistan barely serve to conjure up events so quickly distant and distorted by the passage of time. What other, more delightful memories have I lost through not recording in full those ~~delicious~~ delicate travails in three continents by which at intervals I have been so happily distracted!

My partial recollections of the recent military/campaign somewhat resemble the haunting shapes of those elms that in my childhood loomed from the mists of autumnal Hampshire mornings. There were the overwhelming odours and the rich and rancid flavours of Bombay; the abrupt orders that sent me deep into country threatened by the enemy; the treacherous onslaught of the murderous Ghazis; the shock and confusion of my wounds, my rescue and providential escape before that fearful month-long siege that immured my surviving companions in the fort at Candahar.

How much I regret that I could not share their misfortunes and
the joys of their splendid deliverance by General Bob!

I had, instead, my own ups and downs of fortune: that
painful trek across the border to the hospital at Peshawar;
hopes rising with the healing of my wounds, only to be dashed
by the desperate bout of fever that eventually, for the sake
of my life, persuaded my superiors to despatch me on the railway
a thousand miles south to Karachi, thence to Bombay and finally,
on board the troopship Orontes, back to the safe home of
Portsmouth, whence I made my way to London after visiting old
friends at Netley and relations in Hampshire.

The bare bones of this narrative have sufficed to gather
about me, at several of the bars in London, an interested
circle of listeners, among whom, I am pleased to note, the
ladies in particular have been nicely alarmed by my account.
Only one ~~gentleman~~ scoundrel - I can scarcely call him that - recently
had the impudence to imply that a more precise recollection of
events might have attracted the interest of fewer people. I was
satisfied that the rest of the company avoided the unwelcome
grins and glances with which he tried to enlist their support
for his worthless opinion. Later, this wretched fellow referred
loudly to London as "a great cesspool into which all the
loungers and idlers of the Empire are irresistibly drawn."
I was quick to remark, looking back at him sternly as I left
the Criterion Bar, that the epithet seemed very true, at which
he gave an unattractive laugh and so did several others.

I chose to drink at the Holborn for a number of evenings
after that, which I find more convenient to my purse, and the
walk to High Holborn is no farther from my hotel than the walk
to Piccadilly. My finances at present are stretched to breaking
point, reminiscent of the thin red line of the old British Army
but without the same resilience unfortunately. My lack of
occupation, consequent upon my need for physical recuperation
and a natural desire to revive my spirits in some small pleasures,
is matched by a sorry lack of funds for the purpose, my brother
having appropriated the larger share of those modest resources
made available by our parents' husbandry. I had an unpleasant
exchange with the hotel manager on Saturday, and on Sunday decided
to make a complete alteration in my style of living. Celebrated
my resolve this morning by a return to the Criterion.

Young Stamford was there, to my astonishment, whom I knew
when I was at Bart.'s, before joining the Army. He was a dresser
under me at the hospital but I was never a close friend of ~~never much cared for~~ the man:
a little too pushy with his company. Still, I had not seen him
since those days and felt a duty to respond to his eager
friendliness. I bought him a drink and remarked that we might
share a meal at the Holborn. His manner had improved somewhat
and he was decently impressed by my adventures, which I related
swiftly to him in the cab and over lunch, but this was rather
spoilt, just as I was explaining my urgent need for new
accommodation, when he interrupted to thank me for offering to

pay the bill for both of us, though I knew that I had made no such offer.

On hearing my plans, he was immediately enthusiastic that I should meet an old friend of his called Holmes. I did not like the sound of him. According to Stamford, not only does this fellow beat the subjects in his dissecting room with a stick, to verify how far bruises may be produced after death, but he is, apparently, quite capable of giving his friends a little pinch of the latest vegetable alkaloid merely as a scientific experiment - with fatal possibilities that seemed more to amuse than to concern Stamford. I understood that Holmes is not a medical student but is nonetheless given a free run of the laboratory. It would not have been allowed in my day!

I left Stamford in no doubt that I was suspicious of such attitudes and, when he told me that the fellow was seeking someone to go halves with him in some rooms he had found that were too much for his purse alone, I expressed only mild interest. Stamford continued to be infuriatingly mysterious about the fellow, declared outright that I would probably not get on with. him and had the audacity to imply that it would be my fault if things turned out badly, since it was I who had suggested the meeting in the first place. I replied that I was not yet well enough to stand too much noise and excitement and had no confidence in what I heard. He asked if I would not like, at least, to revisit my old haunts, offered to pay for the cab and so we went.

When we arrived, Stamford was out of the hansom and into
the hospital before the cabman had his hand out for the fare.
I paid, of course, and caught up with my fleet-tongued companion
in the laboratory, which was much as I remembered it, a lofty
chamber, lined and littered with countless bottles. Broad, low
tables were scattered about, which bristled with retorts,
test-tubes and little Bunsen lamps with their blue flickering
flames. There was only one student in the room, who was bending
over a distant table absorbed in his work. He turned and greeted
us with great excitement but I was at once put off when, scarcely
waiting to be introduced, he began talking rapidly about a
discovery he had made of a re-agent which was precipitated by
haemoglobin and nothing else. *How could he claim that, until he had tried everything else?*

I caught the name Holmes but had to ask him to repeat his
first name, which I thought to have misunderstood as Shylock
(the influence of seeing Mr Irving's unusual performance at
the Lyceum!). It was perhaps in pique at my remark that Mr. Sherlock
Holmes shook my hand more vigorously than I was expecting and
tried to impress me by a wild guess that I had recently come
from Afghanistan. I did think this rather clever but had no wish
to further his conceit by saying so.

I was about to entertain him with the benefit of one or
two of my adventures when, to my annoyance, he returned sharply
to the subject of his own experiments, of which he gave a
practical demonstration by digging a long bodkin into his finger
and drawing off the resulting drop of blood in a chemical pipette.

Pouring in a litre of water, he showed us that the mixture had
the appearance of pure water and he stated that the proportion
of blood to water was one to one million but I know this to be
an exaggeration. He then added some white crystals and drops
of an unspecified transparent fluid. The solution changed to a
dull mahogany and a brownish dust was precipitated to the bottom
of the pipette. *The old guaiacum test and the microscope were valueless!*

By this experiment, whether bloodstains were old or new,
Holmes claimed that not only could he distinguish between
obscure dirt and authentic blood but he could thereby bring
about the arrest of many criminals who had thus far eluded the
law. He cited, among those who should not have escaped justice,
Von Bischoff of Frankfort, Mason of Bradford, the notorious
Muller, Lefevre of Montpellier and Samson of New Orleans.

I thought that Holmes showed a child-like delight quite
out of proportion to the incomplete value of the experiment.
He looked to us for applause and I congratulated him in a
deliberately restrained tone but Stamford played up to him and
talked some nonsense about the fellow being "a walking calendar
of crime" and suggested that he should start a paper called
"The Police News of the Past," which appealed to Holmes greatly.

He was sticking a piece of plaster over the prick on his
finger at the time and, seeing my glance, he explained that
he dabbled in poisons quite a bit. He spread out his hands,
showing the patches of plaster and acid stains, as if I had
not been able to observe these for myself when I shook hands

with him or when I watched him at his experiment. I was about
to make a medical remark of some acuity when Stamford brought
up the unwelcome subject of lodgings.

Holmes was interested, to my surprise, for by now I thought
he must be as suspicious of myself as I was of him. He mentioned
a suite in Baker Street, which he had seen, and then cross-examined
me with the apparent intention of putting me off. Irresistibly
I found myself rising to the challenge of this awkward fellow
and matching him squarely. He said he smoked strong tobacco,
so I told him that I smoked "ship's" myself, which I knew to
be the strongest stuff obtainable. He pretended not to mind and
countered with talk of his chemicals and experiments lasting
throughout the night. This was easy for me to dismiss, since
my profession is quite accustomed to such things. Far from
annoying me, I said with satisfaction, this would amuse me
greatly. He mentioned his sulky temperament and was anxious
that we should each confess our worst faults if we were going
to live together, so I told him that I was lazy, objected to
rows and got up at all sorts of ungodly hours, all of which I
believed would be contradictory to his active, argumentative,
domestic requirements.

Stamford seemed amused by this exchange and winked at
Holmes, saying that I had another set of vices when I was well.
I did not object to this hint at the merrier, more sportive
side of my nature and I followed it up by mentioning that
I had a bull-pup. This seemed to strike home and he quickly

Ho(l)me(s)!

referred to his habit of playing the violin. He asked if I
objected and I wittily replied with a catch-phrase I had heard
in the Oxford Music Halls: "A well-played violin is a treat for
the gods - a badly played one . . ." I left the line unfinished,
hoping he would take the point.

Not a bit of it. The fellow laughed, agreed to share with
me and settled we should meet tomorrow at noon to visit the
rooms. Before I could protest at this sudden turn, he had gone
back to his chemicals and was once again immersed in his
experiments, leaving Stamford and myself to make our way out.

As we walked back to my hotel, I could not resist asking
how Holmes might have guessed that I had been in Afghanistan.
Stamford gave an enigmatic reply and said that I was not the
first to be curious as to how Holmes found things out. He made
such a mystery of the man's skills that I was provoked into
demonstrating my own learning by quoting the favourite dictum
of my old professor at Bart.'s, that "the proper study of mankind
is man." Stamford rather spoilt my fun by wagering that Holmes
would learn more about me than I would about him.

I would like to ignore the fellow's suggestion that we
meet tomorrow but on reflection I feel stung to question him
further. That business of Afghanistan still bothers me.

Visited 221B Baker Street with Mr. Sherlock Holmes
Pleasant rooms and good situation at £4 per week to
be shared between the two of us. Concluded agreement
with the landlady, Mrs. Hudson, to take possession
on the spot. Collected trunks from my Hotel, where
I settled my bill most disagreably with the Manager,
and passed the first night alone in Baker Street, with
my bull-pup. I took the opportunity to choose the
bedroom on the floor above our sitting-room, thinking
that would be quieter, and leaving to Holmes the
bedroom next to the sitting-room. Mrs. Hudson and
a maid live on the premises.

Wednesday 12th January.

Holmes spent most of the day moving in with a
large number of boxes and portmanteaux and an
extraordinary collection of bric-a-brac, in which he
expected me to take some interest. Bull-pup
confined to my bedroom during the unloading of
this baggage, with an unfortunate result, which I
have attempted to conceal from Mrs. Hudson.

LONDON

Thursday 13th January.

Holmes still unpacking his trunks and arranging the rooms to his liking. Mrs. Hudson found out about the bull-pup. Made ourselves scarce for the rest of the day.

Friday 14th January.

Holmes decided to rearrange the sitting-room entirely. Perhaps he will be satisfied soon. I do feel that he is making our shared room rather his own, though he is friendly enough. Was it negligence or mischief that caused me accidentally to let the bull-pup out of my bedroom? He ran loose and caused some considerable disturbance among Holmes's books and ornaments. Holmes was not amused, nor was Mrs. Hudson, who took away several chair covers for repair. Holmes muttered something about a fellow's dog that bit his leg when he was at University and I rather fear he might employ some of his vegetable alkaloid to poison the poor creature. Bull-pup will have to go to another home.

30th January 1881

Dear Stamford.

Almost three weeks have passed since my sudden move into these apartments. I cannot forget that it was our chance meeting that brought about my introduction to Holmes and I still do not know whether to praise or to admonish you for your choice of acquaintance. But I thought it proper that I should let you know how we are getting on.

Holmes is reasonably quiet in his ways and his habits are regular — usually in bed before ten and breakfasted and gone out before I rise in the morning. Sometimes he spends his day at the chemical laboratory, sometimes in the dissecting rooms and occasionally in long walks. He is very energetic when the working fit is on him; but now and again a reaction will seize him, and for days on end he will lie upon the sofa in the sitting-room, hardly uttering a word or moving a muscle from morning to night. On these occasions I have noticed such a dreamy, vacant expression in his eyes, that were it not for his apparent temperance I might have suspected him of being addicted to the use of some narcotic!

He certainly has a very striking appearance, and being

so excessively lean, seems taller than his six feet or more. His eyes are sharp and piercing but cloud over during those intervals of torpor. His thin, hawk-like nose gives his whole expression an air of alertness and decision. His chin, too, has the prominence and squareness which mark the man of determination. His hands are invariably blotted with ink and stained with chemicals, yet he is possessed of extraordinary delicacy of touch, as I have often observed.

You may set me down as a hopeless busybody but I would have you remember that my health forbids me to venture out unless the weather is exceptionally genial and so I miss my companions at the Criterion. By the way, Holmes does seem to have rather a lot of visitors himself!

In anticipation of the lunch you promised,

Yours truly

John H. Watson

<u>Saturday, 5th. February, 1881</u>

Holmes out on private business this evening and I have my own
leisure at Baker Street. I am a hopeless fellow to read or
write, whatever my resolve, for I am a great deal too sociable.
The privacy of my bedroom holds few attractions and I am too
damnably curious about Holmes and his activities to sit quietly
with book or pen while he is occupied with something else. The
best time to fill in my notebook is when he is moody or absent
- would that these two features coincided more often!

Since I wrote to Stamford last Sunday I have been much
vexed about my lodging companion. I wrote Stamford a very civil
letter, though several times I have regretted allowing him so
cheekily to act as "marriage" broker. No doubt the fellow was
anxious to avoid being asked to share Baker Street himself.
A spell with Holmes might subdue him mightily! Nor is this
place quite so agreeable as at first I thought. The fireplace
in my bedroom smokes so thickly when the wind is wrong that I
am black all over and like to be taken for an African. There is
certainly no chance of the dark skin I gained in Afghanistan
disappearing swiftly. I am still lost to know how Holmes deduced
that I had been there.

I have also been thinking about Holmes's range of knowledge:
it is a peculiar ragbag of information that he possesses. His
library offers no clue as to what course he has been studying.
It is not medicine, for certain. He has himself confirmed

Stamford's opinion on that point. Neither does he appear to
have any reading that would fit him for a degree in science
or any other recognized portal which would give him an
entrance into the learned world, though he talks at times
as if he has been to both Oxford and Cambridge. I cannot think
that he has completed any course at either one. Yet his zeal
for certain studies is remarkable and within eccentric limits
his knowledge is so extraordinarily ample and minute that his
observations fairly astound me. Surely no man would work so
hard or attain such precise information unless he had some
definite end in view.

Dodgson had just published his second marvellous book when I first dined with him in college

Too many people burden their minds with small matters to no purpose

His ignorance is as remarkable as his knowledge. Of
contemporary literature, philosophy and politics he appears
to know next to nothing. The papers this morning were very
full of the death of Thomas Carlyle yesterday and I took the
liberty of quoting some of Carlyle's words but Holmes made a
great show of naivety, saying that he had never heard of
Carlyle, which I find hard to credit.

Perhaps this is some kind of game or Holmes tires of my
questions? I began to think this when he denied all knowledge
of the Copernican Theory and of the composition of the Solar
System. I do not believe that anyone in the second half of the
Nineteenth Century should not be aware that the Earth travels
round the Sun but Holmes did not seem to care at all if I
thought him the most ignorant man in the world. He made a point
of telling me that he would do his best to forget what I had

just told him. He will accept no advice but his own and seems to have no appreciation of the importance of a proper understanding of the Solar System.

I was about to ask him what did interest him but he was already getting out his violin and I knew that further conversation would be impossible. While he began to tune the strings and to pluck idly at the instrument without at first producing any recognizable line, I thought about all the various points upon which he had said he was exceptionally well informed, remembering that he believed all the knowledge he possessed was such as would be useful to him. I wrote out a list of this knowledge, by which I hoped to deduce what Holmes's real business was but the list was so hopelessly diverse that I threw it into the fire. This was a mistake. The fire flamed up and singed the muffins that were toasting on a fork there.

What else could I do but settle back and listen to Holmes on the violin, which he had started to play properly for once. His powers upon the violin were very remarkable but as eccentric as all his other accomplishments. He could perfectly well play some of my favourite pieces, such as Mendelssohn's "Lieder," at my request, but when left to himself, he would seldom attempt any music or attempt any recognizing air. Leaning back in his armchair of an evening, he would close his eyes and scrape carelessly at the fiddle which was thrown across his knee. Sometimes the chords were sonorous and melancholy.

What the deuce is it to me? You say we go round the Sun. If we went round the moon it would not make a pennyworth of difference to me or to my work.

See my notes at the end of this entry

Occasionally they were fantastic and cheerful. Clearly they
reflected the thoughts which possessed him, but whether the
music aided those thoughts, or whether the playing was simply
the result of a whim or fancy, was more than I could determine.
I might have rebelled against these exasperating solos had it
not been that he usually terminated them by playing in quick
succession a whole series of my favourite airs as a slight
compensation for the trial upon my patience.

* Notes for a paper on the <u>Acquisition of Knowledge</u>

I consider that a man's brain originally is like a little empty attic, and
you have to stock it with such furniture as you choose. A fool takes in all
the lumber of every sort that he comes across, so that the knowledge which
might be useful to him gets crowded out, or at best is jumbled up with a lot of
other things, so that he has difficulty in laying his hands upon it. Now the
skilfull workman is very careful indeed as to what he takes into his brain-attic.
He will have nothing but the tools which may help him in doing his work, but of
these he has a large assortment, and all in the most perfect order.
It is a mistake to think that that little room has elastic walls, and
can distend to any extent. Depend upon it there comes a time when for
every addition of knowledge you forget something that you knew before. It
is of the highest importance, therefore, not to have useless facts elbowing
out the useful ones.

Sunday, 6th February

After foolishly destroying my first list of Holmes's limits, yesterday, I thought it worthwhile to reconstruct the list before I forgot everything:

Sherlock Holmes - his limits

1. Knowledge of Literature : Nil.
2. Knowledge of Philosophy : Nil.
3. Knowledge of Astronomy : Nil.
4. Knowledge of Politics : Feeble.
5. Knowledge of Botany : Variable. Well up in belladonna, opium, and poisons generally. Knows nothing of practical gardening.
6. Knowledge of Geology : Practical but limited. Tells at a glance different soils from each other. After walks has shown me splashes upon his trousers, and told me by their colour and consistence in what part of London he had received them.
7. Knowledge of Chemistry : Profound.
8. Knowledge of Anatomy : Accurate, but unsystematic.
9. Knowledge of Sensational Literature : Immense. He appears to know every detail of every horror perpetrated in the century.
10. Plays the violin well.
11. Is an expert singlestick player, boxer, and swordsman.
12. Has a good practical knowledge of British Law.

Tuesday 8th February

Mr. Lestrade visited Holmes for the third time within
a week. He is a little sallow, rat-faced, dark-eyed
fellow. I have not yet enquired his business. Holmes
again requested the use of the sitting-room for the
afternoon, so I retired to my bedroom having no
money to go out.

Wednesday. 9th February.

Two visitors for Holmes today. In the morning a
young girl, fashionably dressed, who stayed for half-
an-hour or more; in the afternoon, a grey-headed
seedy visitor, looking like a Jew pedlar, much excited
and closely followed by a slip-shod elderly woman.
Of course, I was not wanted, so I took an afternoon
walk in the park and then went to enquire how
my bull-pup was getting along with his new owner.
All is well.

Friday. 11th February.

An old white-haired gentleman for an interview
with Holmes this morning. Saw a galloping show
at the Music Halls in Oxford Street this evening.
Holmes said he was off to the Guildhall Library to
do some research.

Saturday, 12th February,

This is too irritating. I shall demand some explanatio[n]
from Holmes, for I think I have a right to it:
Another visitor again today, a railway porter in his
velveteen uniform. Had to clear out for the fellow, then
Holmes asked very decently and did apologise for his
clients, as he called them. It is a filthy day outside
and my bedroom fireplace is smoking badly.

Monday, 14th February.

St. Valentine's Day cards and keepsakes are quite
the fashion but since my setting up with Holmes I
seem to mix rather less with the ladies than I used
to do. Holmes cheered me up, however, by taking me
to lunch at the Langham, where we met an
interesting young fellow called John Thorndyke, who
wants to set himself up as a barrister and some kind
of expert on medical jurisprudence. He had some
very good stories to tell, and was good enough to
listen to one or two of my own.

Wednesday. 2nd March   1881

This is the third consecutive day on which Holmes
has had visitors. Today it was Mr. Dixon Druce, a
young man who can only have left his private school
about two years ago, I would guess. The talk turned
to scientific and medical subjects but they evidently
did not require my presence. Informed Holmes that
I did not intend to be closetted in my smoke-chamber
for another afternoon and asked him to tell Mrs. Hudson
that I would not be in to supper. He wished me a
jolly good evening. The man can be most ignorant
of the feelings of others! Being at a loss I went
round to the Holborn for a meal, where they had
pineapple for dessert and nothing else, so I ate what
I had. I have detested the fruit since my schooldays,
when I was surrounded by stone pineapples atop every
gate post, placed there because they were a favourite
dish of our school's namesake! Very bad tempered,
I went to the Criterion and tried to recapture some
of the spirit of my freer days but the place was
almost empty. Returned home late, without my
key, but with the pleasant thought that I would have
to wake Holmes to let me in, but to my fury found

that he had himself only just returned from an excellent evening at the Café Royal, and got nothing from him but a cheery, "Back early, nothing doing?"

Thursday, 3rd March.

Up late and felt poorly after those damnable pineapples last night. Spent the morning at the Turkish Baths in Northumberland Avenue and told Mrs. Hudson in a loud voice that I would be spending all afternoon in the sitting-room and would like tea at three-thirty and supper at six-thirty, so that Holmes would be clear that I did not intend to budge. But there were no visitors today and Holmes was in his bedroom all afternoon and evening, keeping very quiet.

Friday, 4th March

The first rain last night for a week. An extraordinary day. My first case with Holmes. The day began by solving the Afghanistan riddle but concluded with the posing of a fiendish murder riddle of far greater mystery. I shall write up a full description in my note-book.

JANUARY 1881

THE BOOK OF LIFE

It has been said accurately that life is an open book, wherein all men may read. Few care to do so. There is nothing in life than an observant man might not learn by an accurate and systematic examination of all that comes in his way. Of all things, his fellow men are the easiest to understand, and no words need pass their lips to help that understanding. A momentary expression, a twitch of a muscle or a glance of an eye will enable any careful observer to fathom a man's inmost thoughts. Words and deeds can be deceptive, but not to one trained to observation and analysis.

Absence of direct information need not itself be any bar to understanding. From a drop of water a logician could infer the possibility of an Atlantic or a Niagara without having seen or heard of one or the other. So all life is a great chain, the nature of which is known whenever we are shown a single link of it. Like all other arts, the Science of Deduction

THE BOOK OF LIFE

and Analysis is one which can only be acquired
by long and patient study, nor is life long enough to
allow any mortal to attain the highest possible
perfection in it. Before turning to these moral and
mental aspects of the matter which present the
greatest difficulties, let the inquirer begin by
mastering more elementary problems. Let him on
meeting a fellow mortal, learn at a glance to
distinguish the history of the man, and the trade or
profession to which he belongs. Puerile as such an
exercise may seem, it sharpens the faculties of
observation, and teaches one where to look and what
to look for. By a man's finger-nails, by his coat-
sleeve, by his boot, by his trouser-knees, by the
callosities of his forefinger and thumb, by his
expression, by his shirt-cuffs — by each of these
things a man's calling is plainly revealed. That all
united should fail to enlighten the competent inquirer
in any case is almost inconceivable.

Consider, for example, the recent case of a man
who had lost his memory and, wishing to regain his
identity, came to me for advice. I was able to help
him, in gratitude for which he afterwards contributed
half a crown to a subscription fund in memory of
the late commander on whose last expedition in
the South Seas. I was able to inform him, he had
taken part. By studying him closely, and without
asking any questions, I was able to deduce that, in
1875, he had been Captain of the Main Top aboard
H.M.S. Pearl in the tragic voyage of Commodore

<u>Friday, 4th. March, 1881</u>

An incident this morning at last cleared up the Afghanistan trick that Holmes played on me when we first met and gave me an insight into his activities. I was up earlier than usual, Holmes was still munching breakfast and while Mrs. Hudson dawdled upon my needs I picked up a magazine and read an article which had been marked with a pencil at the heading.

The article was called "The Book of Life." It attempted to show how much an observant man might learn by an accurate and systematic examination of all that came in his way. It was both shrewd and absurd. Whatever merit the reasoning had, the deductions were clearly far-fetched and the writer made extravagant claims to fathom a man's inner thoughts by the twitch of a muscle or the glance of an eye. Deceit was not possible. Conceit seemed closer to the mark. The writer likened his propositions to those of Euclid and clearly believed that others regarded him as some kind of necromancer.

Ah, the great issues that hang from a boot-lace

I threw down the paper in disgust and remarked that it was ineffable twaddle. While Holmes pretended to ignore me, I added that it was the work of some armchair lounger and that I should like to see him clapped down in a third-class carriage on the Underground and asked to give the trades of all his fellow travellers. I would lay a thousand to one against him, I said.

Holmes waited for me to finish. "I wrote the article myself," he said. I was flabbergasted. Despite my doubts about him, I

had thought him above such ~~fanciful~~ conceptions. [*On the contrary; very practical*] He then showed
me his visiting card (which I had not seen before - with our
new address), on which he called himself a consulting detective.
I cross-questioned him about this, for I thought it time he
gave me a few answers. I asked what the deuce he meant and he
replied that when the Government and private detectives were
at a loss, he put them on the right scent. Did he think he
knew more than them, I queried, to which he made claim that
with the details of a thousand cases at his finger ends, it
would be odd if he couldn't unravel the thousand and first. [*There is a strong family resemblance about misdeeds*]

It was obvious that his visitors were connected with this.
He admitted that Lestrade was a well-known police detective, who
had got himself into a fog recently over a forgery case. The
others had mostly been sent by private enquiry agents. All
were people in trouble who wanted enlightenment. Holmes
boasted that he could often unravel some knot that others
could make nothing of, though they had seen every detail for
themselves. I did not truly believe him. [*I listen to their story; they listen to my comments, and then I pocket my fee*]

I demanded to know who had told him about Afghanistan. [*intuition, special knowledge, deduction and observation*]
He feigned not to hear. "You were told, no doubt," I challenged.
He laughed and said he knew it and then explained the steps in
his reasoning, which I jotted down verbatim:

"Here is a gentleman of a medical type but with the air
of a military man. Clearly an army doctor then. He has just
come from the tropics, for his face is dark, and that is not
the natural tint of his skin, for his wrists are fair. He has

undergone hardship and sickness, as his haggard face says clearly. His left arm has been injured. He holds it in a stiff and unnatural manner. Where in the tropics could an English army doctor have seen much hardship and got his arm wounded? Clearly in Afghanistan." *What about South Africa?*   *No.*

For once, I thought he deserved some credit, so I congratulated him on the simplicity of his solution and *Inferior fellow with some analytical genius. By no* compared him first to Edgar Allen Poe's fictional detective *means such a phenomenon as* Dupin, whose trick of breaking in on his friends' thoughts *Poe imagined* with an apropos remark after a quarter of an hour's silence was showy and superficial, said Holmes immediately, and then to Gaboriau's hero Lecoq, whom Holmes called a bungler whose *Gaboriau's book made me ill—* energy was the only thing to recommend him and who took six *a text book* months to identify an unknown prisoner, a question that would *for detectives to teach* have taken Holmes only twenty-four hours. *them what to avoid*

I was indignant at having two characters whom I admired treated in this cavalier style and I resented Holmes's sardonic air. I turned my back on him and stared out of the window. Clever he may be; conceited he is undoubtedly. He started boasting that one day he would become famous, that no one else had ever put so much study into the detection of crime but there was, alas, no crime to detect or, at most, some bungling villainy with a motive so transparent that even a Scotland *There are no* Yard official could see through it. *crimes and no criminals in these days.*

I knew that I would explode unless I changed the topic, so I brought his attention to a stalwart, plainly-dressed

individual who was walking slowly down the other side of the street, looking anxiously at the numbers. He had a large blue envelope in his hand. Holmes declared him to be a retired sergeant of marines and I was about to reply with "Brag and Bounce, you know you cannot verify your guess," when the fellow crossed the street, knocked on our door, came up the stairs, asked for Holmes and handed him the envelope.

Seizing my opportunity to catch Holmes out, I asked the man what his trade was. He was a commissionaire, he said, but his uniform was away for repairs. I asked him what he had been before. He said, a sergeant, Royal Marine Light Infantry, clicked his heels, saluted and left.

I was confounded, I admit, but convinced the whole thing was pre-arranged, though I felt reluctant admiration for the way in which Holmes had carried it off. As soon as he had finished reading the note, I demanded an explanation. He turned to me with some petulance and said that even across the street he could see a great blue anchor tattooed on the back of the fellow's hand, which smacked of the sea, but knew him to be a marine because of his military carriage and regulation side whiskers. An air of command and self-importance, together with a steady, respectable, middle-aged look indicated that he had been a sergeant. *You must have observed the way in which he held his head and swung his cane*

It was not unreasonable, I thought, but I was surprised to see that Holmes, far from being pleased with himself, was deeply abstracted. He handed me the letter he had received.

Scotland Yard,
            Whitehall.

                                    4th March 188_

My Dear Sherlock Holmes,

There has been a bad business during the night at 3, Lauriston Gardens, off the Brixton Road. Our man on the beat saw a light there about two in the morning, and as the house was an empty one, suspected that something was amiss. He found the door open, and in the front room, which is bare of furniture, discovered the body of a gentleman, well dressed, and having cards in his pocket bearing the name of 'Enoch J. Drebber, Cleveland, Ohio, U.S.A.' There had been no robbery, nor is there any evidence as to how the man met his death. There are marks of blood in the room, but there is no wound upon his person. We are at a loss as to how he came into the empty house; indeed the whole affair is a puzzler. If you can come round to the house any time before twelve you will find me there. I have left everything in statu quo until I hear from you. If you are unable to come, I shall give you fuller details, and would esteem it a great kindness if you would furnish me with an opinion.

            Yours faithfully,

                Tobias Gregson.

Friday, 4th. March, continued

Gregson's note to Holmes stirred me to great excitement but
Holmes was infuriatingly off-hand about the whole business.
He rambled on about Gregson & Lestrade being the pick of
a bad lot of Scotland Yard detectives and obtained much
amusement from telling me what fun there would be if they
were both put upon the case, for they were apparently as
jealous of each other as a pair of professional beauties.

Gregson is the smarter of the two. Both quick and energetic but shockingly conventio

I offered to run for a cab but he seemed wholly indifferent
to any sense of urgency. When I protested that this was just
the sort of case he had been waiting for, he said that, even
if he did unravel the whole matter, Gregson & Lestrade
would pocket all the credit and would never admit that Holmes
had bested them, though they knew well enough that his skill
was superior to theirs.

I can be spry enough at times

That comes from being an unofficial personage

I guessed his diffidence was an act to impress me, for he
suddenly changed his mind, on the excuse that it would amuse
him to beat them at their own game. He seized his overcoat,
told me to come with him and in a minute we were both in a
hansom, heading for the Brixton Road. It was a morning just
such as that described in the adventure story I was reading:
"a foggy, cloudy morning, and a dun-coloured veil hung over
the house-tops, looking like the reflection of the mud-coloured
streets beneath."

Holmes seemed not to have a thought for our business

It is a capital mistake to theorise before you have all the evidence. It biases the judgement

but prattled on about Cremona fiddles and the difference between a Stradivarius and an Amatius. I must admit that I was feeling pretty melancholy because I had thought to have left my share of violence behind me in Afghanistan but Holmes was unperturbed until I pointed out that we must be near the house. The wretched fellow insisted we alight from the cab while we were still a hundred yards away.

Number 3, Lauriston Gardens, was one of four grim looking houses which stood back from the street. Two were occupied but two were empty and a number of "To Let" cards were stuck on several of the windows on all three levels. There was a small garden in front of each house, with some sickly plants and a narrow pathway of clay and gravel made sloppy by last night's rain. A three-foot brick wall topped by wooden rails bounded each garden. A policeman was leaning against the wall, keeping at bay a prying crowd of loafers.

Holmes maintained his affected air of nonchalance, gazed vacantly at the pavement and sauntered along the grass beside the path, staring at the ground. He stopped twice, smiled and uttered an exclamation of ~~self~~-satisfaction. Since there were a great many footsteps on the path, including those of the police, I could not see how he could hope to learn anything from this scrutiny. *My perceptive faculties enable me to see much that is hidden from you*

Gregson greeted us warmly at the door. He was a tall, white-faced, flaxen-haired man, with a notebook in his hand. Holmes at once upbraided him for allowing the police to walk

all over the path but Gregson quickly shifted the blame on to
Lestrade, who was there as well. Holmes teased Gregson that with
two such men on the ground there would not be much for a third
party to find out. Gregson took the remark at face value and
said with pride that he had done all that could be done. He
admitted it was a queer case and had known Holmes's taste for
such things, which was why he had asked him along.

Holmes asked if either man had come by cab. Gregson looked
puzzled and said they had not. We then entered the house by a
short passage, bare-planked and dusty, and turned into a large *It was the dining-*
square room, completely bare of furniture. The wall-paper *room. The paper*
was vulgar
was blotched in places with mildew and peeling to expose the *and flaring*
yellow plaster beneath. Opposite the door was a showy fireplace
imitation
with a mantelpiece of /white marble. On one corner of this was
stuck the stump of a red wax candle. The solitary window was
so dirty that the light was hazy and uncertain, giving a dull
grey tinge to everything, which was intensified by the thick
layer of dust which coated the whole apartment.

The body was lying stretched out and face upwards on the
boards. It was that of a man in his early forties, middle-sized,
broad-shouldered, with tight curly black hair and a short,
stubbly beard. He was dressed in a heavy broadcloth frock coat
and waistcoat, with light-coloured trousers, and immaculate
collar and cuffs. A top hat, well brushed and trim, was placed
upon the floor beside him. His hands were clenched and his arms
thrown abroad, while his lower limbs were interlocked, as though

his death struggle had been a grievous one. On his rigid face there stood an expression of horror, and, as it seemed to me, of hatred, such as I have never seen upon human features. This malignant and terrible contortion, combined with the low forehead, blunt nose, and prognathus jaw, gave the dead man a singularly simious and ape-like appearance, which was increased by his writhing, unnatural posture. I have seen death in many forms, but never has it appeared to me in a more fearsome aspect than in that dark, grimy apartment, which looked out upon one of the main arteries of suburban London.

Avoid sensationalism

Holmes pointed to the bloodstains around the body and asked if the detectives were sure there was no wound. Both were positive. Holmes then made much of stating that the blood came from someone else, possibly the murderer, which seemed pretty obvious. He examined the dead man swiftly, sniffed his lips, glanced at the soles of his patent-leather boots, asked if he had been moved and when told, no more than necessary, advised Gregson to remove the body.

Compare van Jansen, Utrecht, 1834. There is nothing new under the sun. It has all been done before

As it was being raised, a ring tinkled down and rolled across the floor. Lestrade grabbed it and declared it to be a plain gold woman's wedding ring. Gregson exclaimed that this made matters even more complicated than they were before but Holmes said it made things simpler. Both men stared at him blankly. He did not explain. He asked to see the contents of the dead man's pockets. Gregson showed him a litter of objects on the stairs and handed him a list of items.

He was convinced there had been a woman in the house

Lauriston Gardens
4th March 1881

Horseshoe and
carriage tracks
in road .

Lauriston Gardens
4th March 1881

Footprints on
Garden Path

Lanriston Gardens
4th March 1881

Enoch J. Drubber

GUION LINE

| 5, Waterloo-place, | 25, Water-street, | 11, Rumford-street, |
| Pall-mall, S.W., London. | Liverpool. | Liverpool. |

Mr. E.J. Drebber,   28th. February, 1881

c/o American Exchange,

Strand,

S.W., London

Dear Sir,

      In accordance with your request, we have reserved a
passage for you on board our regular weekly mail steamer service
from Liverpool to New York, sailing from Liverpool on Saturday,
5th. March. For further details of the vessel and time of
departure, we beg that you will contact our Pall-mall office.

      We like to remind our passengers that the service
supplies abundant provisions of excellent quality served and
cooked by the company's stewards. We are proud to boast that
the Guion Line has not lost a single English, Welsh, Scotch
or Irish passenger for the last 25 years. We wish you a very
pleasant voyage, and respectfully remain yours.

      on behalf of the Guion Line,

Guion Line

Metropolitan Police.

Brixton STATION.   W   DIVISION

4th March 1881

Particulars of
Occurrence reported
by Constable Rance

Case Referred to
Detectives Gregson
and Lestrade

Effects of Enoch J. Drebber, found on his body at
3 Lauriston Gardens, Brixton.

Gold Watch, No. 97163, by Barraud, of London.

Gold Albert Chain, very heavy and solid.

Gold ring, with Masonic device.

Gold pin, bull-dog's head, with ruby eyes.

Russian leather card case, with cards, Enoch J. Drebber of Cleveland

Linen handkerchief, marked with E.J.D.

Loose money, £7. 13/-

* Pocket edition of the Decameron, Boccaccio, published by Chatto
and Windus, London, 1874, with name of Joseph Stangerson on
fly leaf

Two letters addressed to E.J. Drebber and Joseph Stangerson,
both marked to be left at the American Exchange, Strand,
till called for, both from the Guion Steamship Company,
with reference to the sailing of their boats from Liverpool
to New York, Saturday, 5th March.

Wedding ring, woman's, plain gold.

* Note that this is the complete translation
with an Introduction by Thomas Wright
restoring those passages omitted in
former editions. Drebber's choice
or Stangerson's?

Joseph Wrigley (Sgt.)

Friday, 4th. March, continued

When Holmes had inspected the dead man's effects in the hallway, Gregson informed him with some satisfaction that he had already placed an advertisement for Stangerson in all the evening papers, that one of his men had gone to make enquiries at the American Exchange and that he had telegraphed Cleveland asking for further information on both Drebber & Stangerson. Holmes at once unsettled the detective by suggesting he had overlooked a crucial point and by asking if he would not care to telegraph again. Gregson was not amused, thinking that Holmes was merely joking at his expense.

Lestrade then reappeared from the front room, rubbing his hands in a pompous and self-satisfied manner. He added to Gregson's discomfort by declaring that he had made a discovery of the utmost importance. We followed him back into the room, where he led us to the darkest corner, struck a match on his boot, held it up against the wall to an area where a large piece of paper had peeled off, leaving a yellow square of coarse plastering, and revealed, scrawled in blood-red letters, a single word: "RACHE." *He had the air of a showman exhibiting his show.*

The little fellow looked to us for congratulation and, with a triumphant glance at Gregson, made it obvious that no-one else had thought of searching in that corner. He pointed to the smear of blood that had trickled down the wall and said

that the murderer had obviously written it with his or her *He no doubt observed that had the candle on the mantelpiece nearby been lit at the time of the murder this corner of the room would have been the brightest instead of the darkest.*

own blood, thus disposing of any idea of suicide. Gregson

was determined not to lose face entirely but when he asked,

with evident disapproval, what the word meant now that Lestrade

had found it, his rival bounced back eagerly and claimed that

whoever had done it had been disturbed before completing the

word "RACHEL" and that a woman of that name would certainly *He accused me of being very smart and clever, but snapped that the old hound was best when all was said and done.*

be found to be involved in the case eventually. Holmes burst

out laughing and then tried to placate the offended detective

by giving him the credit for discovering the word. He asked

for permission to examine the room more carefully.

Holmes had so far appeared rather casual about everything

but now I was fascinated to watch him work with fierce

concentration. He whipped a tape measure and a large round

magnifying glass from his pocket and with these two implements

he trotted noiselessly about the room, sometimes stopping,

occasionally kneeling, and once lying flat upon his face. So

engrossed was he with his occupation that he appeared to have

forgotten our presence, for he chattered away to himself under

his breath the whole time, keeping up a running fire of

exclamations, groans, whistles, and little cries suggestive

of encouragement and hope. As I watched him I was irresistibly

reminded of a pure-blooded, well-trained foxhound as it dashes

backwards and forwards through the covert, whining in its

eagerness, until it comes across the lost scent. For twenty

minutes or more he continued his researches, measuring with the

most exact care marks which were entirely invisible to me, and occasionally applying his tape to the walls in an equally incomprehensible manner. In one place he gathered up very carefully a little pile of grey dust from the floor, and packed it away in an envelope. Finally he examined with his glass the word upon the wall, going over every letter of it with the most minute exactness. This done, he appeared to be satisfied, for he replaced his tape and his glass in his pocket.

Gregson & Lestrade asked with curiosity and some contempt what he made of it and Holmes replied that they were doing so well it would be a pity for anyone to interfere. He took down the name and address of John Rance, the constable who had found the body, and then made a bold statement that the murderer was a man, more than six feet high, in the prime of life, with small feet for his height, wearing coarse, square-toed boots and smoking a Trichinopoly cigar. He had come with his victim in a four-wheeled cab, which was drawn by a horse with three old shoes and one new one on his off foreleg. In all probability the murderer had a florid face and the finger-nails of his right hand were remarkably long.

Neither man believed a word of it, for they shook their heads and smiled at each other; nor did I but if it was a bluff I thought it a very good one. Gregson asked how the murder had been done and Holmes replied it was poison. To Lestrade, he said, "RACHE" was the German for "Revenge;" so to look for Miss Rachel would be a waste of time. We left both men open-mouthed.

Lauriston Gardens
4th March 1887

FORM FOR AMERICAN MESSAGES ONLY

No. of Message **5491**

Station **Brixton**

Prefix **SY/MP** Code Time **0832** WORDS TO BE SIGNALLED. **64**

Message ....

Received **0828** m }
Finished **0832** m }

Date **4th March** 187

Repeating **Account of**

Sent to **CLEVELAND** Station.

Reply .... **Scotland Yard**

by me **Enoch** Clerk.

To be paid out ... ,, ,,

(DQ—MM)   (Address)   (MM—PQ)

Counter Clerk's Initials ...... } **AK**

Total ...... ,, ,,

FROM

Name and Address of the Sender of the Message.
{ **GREGSON SCOTLAND YARD LONDON** }

TO

Name and Full Address of the Person to whom the Message is to be delivered.
{ **POLICE HEADQUARTERS CLEVELAND OHIO USA** }

DQ

BODY IDENTIFIED AS ENOCH J DREBBER OF
CLEVELAND OHIO USA DISCOVERED THIS MORNING AT
THREE LAURISTON GARDENS BRIXTON LONDON STOP
SUSPECTED FOUL PLAY STOP EVIDENCE OF ASSOCIATION WITH
JOSEPH STANGERSON NOT YET APPREHENDED STOP BOTH
MEN DUE TO TAKE GUION LINE LIVERPOOL TO NEW YORK
LEAVING LIVERPOOL SATURDAY FIFTH MARCH STOP
PLEASE TELEGRAPH ANY PREVIOUS CRIMINAL
RECORD ON DREBBER OR STANGERSON STOP URGENT
STOP

THIS MESSAGE IS PAID FOR AS AN ORDINARY UNPACKED MESSAGE.

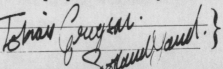

NOTICE TO THE PUBLIC.

CONDITIONS AS TO MESSAGES TO AMERICA.

The Companies to which the American Cables belong will not incur or accept any liability whatsoever, either for the due transmission of Telegrams to the Cables, or for their safe delivery at their destination ; nor will they accept any liability arising from delay or stoppage by reason of any accident to the Cables or Instruments, or from errors caused by indistinct handwriting, nor will they consent to be liable, under any circumstances, for any sum whatever, as damages or otherwise, for loss resulting from errors, mistakes, delays, or other causes in respect to any Message entrusted to them, beyond the return of that portion of the charge accruing to them out of the amount received, and then only in case the Message should fail in transmission when in their hands.

SOLE IMPRESSIONS

A MONOGRAPH

ON

The tracing of footsteps with some
remarks upon the use of plaster of
Paris as a preserver of impresses.

BY

SHERLOCK HOLMES

LONDON

JOHN VAN VOORST, PATERNOSTER ROW

1879

SOLE IMPRESSIONS

It is the intention of this small paper to put forward certain suggestions for the improvement of police methods in the identification and casting of footprints and to provide official detectives with information which may enable them to draw their own comparisons and deductions.

I do not expect to change their methods quickly. The average police constable shows little regard for the valuable information in the pursuit of a criminal that can be gained from preserving and studying an impression. I have seen innumerable cases in which qualified detectives have made comparisons of footprints by placing their boot or shoe *over* the footmark which has been discovered, thus *obliterating* it, rather than making a *new impression* by the side of the original.

The use of plaster of Paris is generally recommended by the police for the taking of impressions but this is not a satisfactory method. Such impressions are often too rough and coarse to be of much service. Casts are practically useless as evidence unless they faithfully correspond with the object modelled. A mere similarity in the sole of a boot or shoe, with a footmark, is of little or no value in evidence; a striking peculiarity must be detected to render such resemblance valid; such as the loss of a nail, or nails, of a plate, or a piece of a plate, or some other peculiarity or corresponding irregularity, which may identify beyond a doubt the footmarks with the boots or shoes compared with them.

I have already suggested to a police adviser, who is himself an inventor, Dr. Moss, the use of a new composition which will give easily and accurately models of such impressions in their finest detail. This preparation consists of resin mixed with wax or paraffin in suitable proportions, whereby is obtained at a small cost a compound which becomes quite fluid at a temperature below the boiling point of water, and which becomes hard and tough on cooling and may without injury to the impression be washed clean from adhering foreign matter with water.

I have no doubt that Dr. Moss will take the credit for the use of this composition but I believe that it will take ten or fifteen years for the process to be accepted officially by the police. I would venture to suggest that even in the last two or three years of this century the average Constable's Pocket Book will still contain instructions for the use of plaster of Paris! Far from considering myself to be an outraged victim of the plagiarist, I would be well satisfied if the police would draw up a paper of their own based verbatim on some of the ideas expressed in this Monograph. Imitation is a singular form of flattery.

It is noteworthy that this composition will also facilitate the taking of casts of a track found upon inclined ground. I have watched on countless occasions the long face of a constable or detective observing his plaster of Paris pouring out of the lower end of the print, when he has not taken care to ridge that end first with clay. Using the composition, the print can be filled by degrees, and the mixture in the lower end of the print will cool quickly, allowing more to be added to fill the upper end.

Further to these matters, a major concern of this Monograph is to introduce to the police some concept of the stride pattern that can be deduced from footprints and the further deductions that can be made from this. Not only can a man's height be ascertained from the length of his stride, but also his weight and his state of health.

ASHES TO ASHES

A MONOGRAPH

ON

The Distinction Between the
Ashes of the Various Tobaccos
in which
One hundred and forty forms of cigar,
cigarette, and pipe tobacco are
enumerated, with colour plates
illustrating the difference in the ash.

BY

SHERLOCK HOLMES

LONDON

JOHN VAN VOORST, PATERNOSTER ROW

1880

Abstract of Contents

1 Tables of cigar, cigarette and pipe tobaccos, with analysis of resultant ash of each type, its colour, texture and odour.

2 Characteristic behaviour of individuals, interpreted through the paraphernalia and residue of their smoking habits :
 i) Analysis of lung strength, with reflection on physical condition, as determined by the length of cigar ash, with reference to the durability and burning speed of a range of tobaccos.
 ii) Analysis of cigar and cigarette stubs, with particular reference to saliva and inferences therefrom.
 iii) Analysis of individual character from the teeth marks in pipe stems, with further reference to the age and health of the smoker, and a variety of habits.

3 Current trends are examined in popular smoking habits and in fashionable attitudes to cigars and cigarettes :
 i) Analysis of the latest record of the smoking habits of the populace in the recent decade; over half the tobacco smoked in our towns being in the form of cigars; reference to importer's list of 1870, showing more than 66 different sizes and brands of cigar, excluding Bengall cheroots, or the much cheaper 1d cigars.
 ii) Popular fads and the effect on cigars; belief that the lightest colour 'claro' is necessarily the mildest, whereas it is the least mature; effect of this belief on manufacturers, who now use the light wrappers almost to the complete exclusion of the darker, more mature ones.

4 Thrip, fog's eye, pole sweat, cut worms and cigarette beetle : diseases of tobacco prevalent in certain areas of the world and the effects of treatment identifiable in cigars and cigarettes manufactured from these areas.

5   A review of the areas of tobacco growing throughout the world with particular emphasis on certain lesser known idiosyncracies :

  i) Variations in the regional types of Turkish "tumbeki" or Narquileh tobacco. used in the "hubble-bubble."

  ii) Variations imposed by the use of different species of evergreen oaks (*Quercus* spp.) when burning their leafy branches to provide smoke for 7–9 month fumigation necessary to give distinctive Latakia tobacco from the province of Saida in northern Syria its black colour and peculiar flavour.

  iii) Development of recent (1862) tobacco industry in Sumatra ; better suited to wrappers than filler ; with assessment of weight of bales and particular weight variation when used for the smuggling of certain goods.

  iv) Cultivation of tobacco in Bombay. Madras and the Punjab, with suggestions for use of American experts to superintend estates and factories ; especial reference to Trichinopoly area of Madras Presidency and inferior quality of some of the tobacco from that area (dark and flakey). and in consequence of the poor conditions of soil.

  v) Suggestions for the development of tobacco industry in British North Borneo ; soil conditions should provide cigar wrappers as good as those in Sumatra ; planters can seek new lands free from the heavy taxation to which they are subjected in Sumatra ; inevitability of planters beginning cultivation within 2–3 years.

6   Lancaster, Pennsylvania and Hartford. Connecticut : detailed analysis of less abundant elements of plant nutrients used in test plots of tobacco in these areas. Initial tests having proved" elementary and inadequate. it is recommended that they be retaken officially at regular intervals. It is to be hoped that there will be no great delay in this research.

Friday, 4th. March, continued

We left Lauriston Gardens at one o'clock. Holmes sent a long
telegram, which he refused to show me, and then insisted that
we took a cab to 46, Audley Court, Kennington Park Gate,
where Constable Rance lived. I asked bluntly whether he was
as sure of his facts as he made out and he at once launched
into such a plausible explanation that I felt quite guilty.

My mind was made up but I thought we might as well obtain some first-hand evidence

The first thing, he said, he had observed at Lauriston
Gardens was that a cab had made two ruts with its wheels close
to the kerb. Since, up to last night, we had had no rain for
a week, those wheels which left such a deep impression must
have been there during the night.* Therefore it brought the
two individuals to the house. There were the marks of the
horse's hoofs, too, the outline of one of which was far more
clearly cut than that of the other three, showing that there
was a new shoe.

I have Gregson's word for it that no cab arrived in the morning

I said that was simple enough but asked about the other
man's height. Holmes explained that the height of a man, in
nine cases out of ten, can be told from the length of his
stride. This fellow's stride was evident on the clay outside
and on the dust within. The calculation could be checked, he
said, for when a man writes on a wall, his instinct leads him
to write about the level of his own eyes, and that writing
was just over six feet from the ground.

A simple calculation no use boring you with figures

Child's play!

How about his age, I asked. Holmes replied that if a man

could stride four and a half feet without the slightest effort,
he couldn't be quite in the sere and yellow. That was the *No mystery simply the application of basic precepts of observation and deduction*
breadth of a puddle on the path which he had evidently
walked across. Patent-leather boots had gone round, and
Square-toes had hopped over, claimed Holmes.

The finger-nails and the Trichinopoly, I said. Holmes
answered that the writing on the wall was done with a man's
forefinger dipped in blood. His glass had allowed him to
observe that the plaster was slightly scratched in doing it,
which would not have been the case if the man's nail had been
trimmed. He had also gathered up some scattered ash from the *It is in such details that the skilled detective differs from Gregson and Lestrade*
floor. It was dark in colour and flaky - such as was only
made by Trichinopoly, said Holmes, who claimed that he could
distinguish at a glance the ash of any known brand either of
cigar or of tobacco.

I asked about the florid face but Holmes admitted that
was a more daring shot and would not answer. The case seemed *I had no doubt that I was right*
no less mysterious to me for all his glib replies. How came
these two men into an empty house? What became of the cabman
who drove them? How could one man compel another to take
poison? Where did the blood come from? What was the object of
the murderer, since robbery had no part in it? How came the
woman's ring there? Above all, why should the second man
write up the German word "RACHE" before decamping? Holmes
acknowledged that there were still a few obscure points but
believed this last to be merely a ruse to put the police on

the wrong track, for a real German would have printed in Latin

characters and not used a clumsy imitation German "A."

Holmes then put on a rather bad show of diffidence and

refused to tell me anything more about his method of working,

in case, he said, I concluded that he was a very ordinary *A conjuror gets*

no credit once

individual after all. I did not want him to stop and, since *he has*

explained

I had already observed that he was as sensitive to flattery *his trick*

on the score of his art as any girl could be of her beauty,

I told him that he had brought detection as near an exact

science as it ever would be brought in this world.

He flushed with pleasure, told me that Patent-leathers

and Square-toes had arrived in the same cab and had walked

aim in aim probably

down the path as friendly as possible. Inside, Patent-leathers *I could*

read this

stood still while Square-toes walked up and down, growing more *in the*

shown by the increased length of his strides *dust*

excited, talking all the time, and working himself into a fury.

Then the tragedy occurred. That was all he knew, said Holmes,

but it was a good basis on which to start. *The rest is mere surmise and*

conjecture

Our cab meanwhile passed through dingy byways and stopped

outside a narrow passageway. We walked into a paved quadrangle,

lined by sordid dwellings, cluttered by dirty children and

discoloured linen, until we came to the name "RANCE" engraved

on the door of Number 46. We were shown into the parlour and

the constable appeared from bed, grumbling that he had made his

report at the office. He changed his tune when Holmes started

playing with a half-sovereign and said we wanted to hear it all

from his own lips. I took down everything he said verbatim.

Unofficial conversation with Constable Rance

John Rance: I'll tell it ye from the beginning. My time is from
ten at night to six in the morning. At eleven there was a fight
at the White Hart; but bar that all was quiet enough on the
beat. At one o'clock it began to rain, and I met Harry Murcher
- him who has the Holland Grove beat - and we stood together at
the corner of Henrietta Street a-talkin'. Presently - maybe
about two or a little after - I thought I would take a look
round and see that all was right down the Brixton Road. It was
precious dirty and lonely. Not a soul did I meet all the way
down, though a cab or two went past me. I was a-strollin' down,
thinkin' between ourselves how uncommon handy a four of hot gin
would be, when suddenly the glint of a light caught my eye in
the window of that same house. Now, I knew that them two houses
in Lauriston Gardens was empty on account of him that owns them
who won't have the drains seed to, though the very last tenant
what lived in one of them died o' typhoid fever. I was knocked
all in a heap, therefore, at seeing a light in the window, and
I suspected as something was wrong. When I got to the door -

Holmes: (interrupting) You stopped and then walked back
to the garden gate. What did you do that for?

Rance: (startled) Why, that's true, sir, though how you
come to know it, Heaven only knows. Ye see when I got up to the
door, it was so still and lonesome, that I thought I'd be none
the worse for someone with me. I ain't afeard of anything on

this side o' the grave; but I thought that maybe it was him that died o' the typhoid inspecting the drains what killed him. The thought gave me a kind o' turn, and I walked back to the gate to see if I could see Murcher's lantern, but there wasn't no sign of him nor of anyone else.

Holmes: There was no one in the street?

Rance: Not a livin' soul, sir, nor as much as a dog. Then I pulled myself together and went back and pushed the door open. All was quiet inside, so I went into the room where the light was a-burnin'. There was a candle flickerin' on the mantelpiece - a red wax one - and by its light I saw -

Holmes: Yes, I know all that you saw. You walked round the room several times, and you knelt down by the body, and then you walked through and tried the kitchen door, and then -

Rance: (springing up in alarm) Where was you hid to see all that? It seems to me that you knows a deal more than you should.

Holmes: (laughing and showing his card) Don't go arresting me for the murder. I am one of the hounds and not the wolf; Mr. Gregson or Mr. Lestrade will answer for that. Go on, though. What did you do next?

Rance: (sitting down, mystified) I went back to the gate and sounded my whistle. That brought Murcher and two more to the spot.

Holmes: Was the street empty then?

Rance: Well, it was, as far as anybody that could be of any good goes.

Holmes: What do you mean?

Rance: (grinning) I've seen many a drunk chap in my time but never anyone so cryin' drunk as that cove. He was at the gate when I came out, a-leanin' up ag'in the railings, and a-singin' at the pitch o' his lungs about Columbine's New-fangled Banner, or some such stuff. He couldn't stand, far less help.

Holmes: (intently) What sort of man was he?

Rance: (irritated) He was an uncommon drunk sort o' man. He'd ha' found hisself in the station if we hadn't been so took up.

Holmes: (impatiently) His face - his dress - didn't you notice them?

Rance: I should think I did notice them, seeing that I had to prop him up - me & Murcher between us. He was a long chap, with a red face, the lower part muffled round -

Holmes: (exasperated) That will do. What became of him?

Rance: We'd enough to do without lookin' after him. I'll wager he found his way home all right.

Holmes: How was he dressed?

Rance: A brown overcoat.

Holmes: Had he a whip in his hand?

Rance: A whip - no.

Holmes: He must have left it behind. You didn't happen to see or hear a cab after that?

Rance: No.

(End of conversation)

Holmes handed the constable the half-sovereign and told
him that he would never rise in the force and that his head
should be for use as well as ornament. He might have gained
his sergeant's stripes last night, said Holmes, for the man
he held in his hands was the man who holds the clue of this
mystery and whom we are seeking. *There was no use arguing about it. I told him it was so.*

We left our informant thoroughly perplexed. Holmes was
very angry that the man had missed his one bit of luck and I
said that I was rather surprised that the criminal, who fitted
Holmes's description so well, had returned to the scene of the
crime. Holmes said it was the ring for which he'd come back
and he bet two to one he'd catch the man by using the ring for
bait. I was rather pleased when he thanked me for persuading
him to respond to Gregson's call, especially when he said *A little art jargon*
that he might otherwise have missed one of the finest studies
he'd ever come across. A study in scarlet, he called it, musing
on the scarlet thread of murder that runs through the colourless
skein of life. *Our duty is to unravel it, and isolate it, and expose every inch of it.*

Holmes then became more positive and began to look *Her attack and her bowing are splendid*
forward to a Norman-Neruda concert he was attending in the
afternoon. (I was suspicious of this, because I knew that
these "Popular Concerts" were only on Mondays and Saturdays!*)
He leant back in the cab and started singing a little tune *The tune was Chopin, and you have*
that went something like Tra-la-la-lira-lira-lay, but I may
have got it wrong. And so we returned to Mrs. Hudson's lunch
at Baker Street.

*This was a special rehearsal for
the last performance of the season.*

The receipt of this
form need not be
acknowledged.

METROPOLITAN POLICE.

Brixton Station, W Division.

4th March 1871 .

PARTICULARS OF AN OCCURRENCE.

(N.B.—This is not a copy of a Police Report, but merely an abstract of such particulars as may be useful to
persons concerned. See Memorandum printed overleaf.)

Date *4th March, 1881*

Place *No 3 Lauriston Gardens, Brixton*

Name and Number of Police Officer who reported the occurrence, stating whether
or not he was a witness:— *Constable Rance W45*

Not a witness

Names and addresses of witnesses :— *None*

a fight, without resistance, at the White Front public-house at eleven. Exchanged important information with Constable Munchin at one o'clock. It began to rain. Shortly after two o'clock, alerted by light in window of No. 3. Lauriston Gardens, known to be an empty house. Entered immediately and discovered unattended candle burning in front room. Observed body of man lying on floor. Confined that gentleman was deceased and checked room for other persons. Went directly to road and sounded whistle. Constable Munchin and two others answered my call. No suspicious persons found in premises or in immediate vicinity. Handed over the case to detectives Gregson and Lestrade.

Signature of Station Officer

Counter-signature of Superintendent

Forwarded, by direction of the Commissioner of Police of the Metropolis, to Detectives Gregson and Lestrade in compliance with 6/2 application of the 4th inst.

New Scotland Yard, S.W.
5th March ____, 188_

T. A. ____
Chief Clerk.

Sherlock Holmes
London 1878

METROPOLITAN POLICE

INSTRUCTION BOOK

FOR THE USE OF

CANDIDATES AND CONSTABLES

OF THE

METROPOLITAN POLICE FORCE.

LONDON:
PRINTED BY G. E. EYRE AND WILLIAM SPOTTISWOODE,
PRINTERS TO THE QUEEN'S MOST EXCELLENT MAJESTY.
FOR HER MAJESTY'S STATIONERY OFFICE.

1871.

Introduction.

THE object of this little book is to give the Candidates on the Preparatory Class and inexperienced Constables some information respecting the service they are entering, and to point out in easy and simple language a few general rules for their guidance.

The Police Orders issued from time to time on very many subjects are voluminous and extensive, and it is well that the young beginner should not be distracted by attempting to grasp too much at one time, and so perhaps become alarmed at all that he may suppose is required of him; but rather that he should read the following pages as the first lessons and advice, which he can easily understand; and if he follows them strictly, he may rest assured he will meet few difficulties he cannot readily surmount.

Metropolitan Police Office,
4, Whitehall Place, and
Scotland Yard, London.
4th May 1871.

When called upon by a person to take another person into custody, he must be guided in a great measure by the circumstances of the case, such as the position in life of the accuser and the accused, and the nature of the charge or offence; but if he has any doubt as to how he ought to act, the safest course is to ask all the persons concerned to go with him to the Station, where the Inspector will hear and determine whether the charge is to be entered or not, and the responsibility is then taken off the Constable.

Perfect command of temper is indispensable. A man must not allow himself to be moved or excited by any language or threats, however violent; the cooler he keeps himself the more power he will have over his assailants. Idle or silly remarks are unworthy of notice, and if the persons making them see that they have no effect upon the Constable they will soon leave off.

In apprehending a person, and making him or her a prisoner, no more violence is to be used than is absolutely necessary for the safe custody of the prisoner. The usual plan is to take hold of the arm and to keep hold until the prisoner is in the station.

14

If a prisoner resists, the constable is bound to struggle with him and overpower him, but not injure him unnecessarily. If the Constable is likely to be overpowered he may draw his truncheon and use it, taking care to avoid striking anyone on the head. The arms and legs should be aimed at to disable a prisoner, as parts of the frame least likely to suffer serious injury. He may also spring his rattle which will bring assistance. These extreme measures are not to be resorted to except in extreme cases when all other attempts have failed, and a prisoner is likely to escape through the constable being ill-used and overpowered.

In such cases as the following a Constable must act with energy, promptness, and determination, for if he wavers, or doubts, the thief may escape, or the opportunity to render assistance may be lost. If a felony has been committed, and the thief is seen, he must be at once apprehended; or if the Constable receives information that a serious crime has been or is about to be committed, he must go at once to the spot and prevent violence, or apprehend the offender if the crime is committed.

If an accident occurs and any person is injured or insensible, he must send some one

Our morning's exertions had been too much for my weak health,
and I was tired out in the afternoon. After Holmes's departure
for the concert, I lay down upon the sofa and endeavoured to
get a couple of hours' sleep. It was a useless attempt. My mind
had been too much excited by all that had occurred, and the
strangest fancies and surmises crowded into it. Every time that
I closed my eyes I saw before me the distorted, baboon-like
countenance of the murdered man. So sinister was the impression
which that face had produced upon me that I found it difficult
to feel anything but gratitude for him who had removed its
owner from the world. If ever human features bespoke vice of
the most malignant type, they were certainly those of Enoch J.
Drebber, of Cleveland. Still, justice must be done.

The more I thought of it the more *extraordinary* ~~absurd~~ did my companion's
hypothesis, that the man had been poisoned, appear. I remembered
how he had sniffed his lips, and had no doubt that he had
detected something which had given rise to the idea. Then,
again, if not poison, what had caused the man's death, since
there was neither wound nor marks of strangulation? But, on the
other hand, whose blood was that which lay so thickly upon the
floor? There were no signs of a struggle, nor had the victim
any weapon with which he might have wounded an antagonist.
As long as all these questions were unsolved, sleep was no easy
matter for me - and should not be for Holmes. *Not so - I had already formed a theory which explained all the facts*

He was very late in returning - so late that I knew that
the concert could not have detained him all the time. Dinner
was on the table before he appeared but the first thing he
was anxious to do was to tell me how magnificent the music
had been. He was full of some rather broad nonsense about
Darwin's claim that the power of producing and appreciating
music existed among the human race long before the power of
speech was arrived at. Holmes suggested that was the reason
why we are so subtly influenced by music but I told him that
this meant very little to me. *There are vague memories in our souls of those misty centuries when the world was in its childhood*

One's ideas must be as broad as nature. if they are to interpret Nature

Holmes brought the subject back to Brixton and suggested
that the affair was upsetting me. I said that it was but then
I thought it as well to remind him how I had seen my own
comrades hacked to pieces in Maiwand without losing my nerve
during the Afghan war. I think he took my point, because he
began to talk about mystery stimulating the imagination,
which seemed to show that he appreciated my relish for the
curious and the unconventional.

Where there is no imagination there is no honor.

Then he passed me the evening paper and showed me an
account of the affair, pointing out that it did not mention
the fact that when the man was raised up a woman's wedding-ring
had fallen on the floor. He seemed to think this omission was
just as well and he drew my attention to an advertisement
which directed anyone who had lost a wedding-ring in the
Brixton Road to apply to Dr. Watson at 221B Baker Street,
apologized for using my name and explained that if he had used

his own some dunderheads would recognize it and want to meddle
in the affair. I said that I had no ring and he handed me a
perfect facsimile. I asked whom he expected to answer the
advertisement and he said, the man in the brown coat - our
florid friend with the square toes, he called him - or some
accomplice. I suggested that the man might think it rather *I had already every reason to believe that it was*
dangerous but Holmes explained that, if his view of the case
was correct, the fellow would rather risk anything than lose
the ring. He outlined his reasoning.

According to Holmes, the fellow dropped the ring while
stooping over Drebber's body, and did not miss it at the time.
After leaving the house he discovered his loss and hurried
back, but found the police already in possession, owing to his
own folly in leaving the candle burning. He had to pretend to
be drunk in order to allay the suspicions which might have
been aroused by his appearance at the gate. Now put yourself
in that man's place, said Holmes. On thinking the matter over,
it must have occurred to him that it was possible that he had
lost the ring in the road after leaving the house. What would
he do then? He would eagerly look out for the evening papers
in the hope of seeing it among the articles found. His eye,
of course, would alight upon the advertisement. He would be
overjoyed. Why should he fear a trap? There would be no reason
in his eyes why the finding of the ring should be connected
with the murder. He would come. He will come, promised Holmes.
We should see him within an hour.

I asked, what would happen then, and he said that I could
leave it to him but suggested I should clean and load my old
service revolver in case he proved to be a desperate man.
I did so and returned to the sitting-room to find him scraping
his violin and gloating over an answer to his American telegram,
which again he would not show me but which, he claimed, proved
that his view of the case was entirely correct.

He then complained that his fiddle would be the better
for new strings and told me to put my pistol in my pocket and
to act naturally when the fellow arrived, leaving everything
to Holmes. The advertisement had said to come between eight
and nine. When we realized that it was eight already, Holmes
asked me to open the door slightly and put the key on the inside.

As was his nature, he began to talk about something
completely different, to cover his own excitement. He showed
me a book he had picked up at a stall the day before and
made some fearful joke about Charles's head still being firm
on his shoulders when the little brown-backed volume was
struck off. To cover the fact that I was myself far too
excited to catch the name of the book, I asked who printed
it and missed the answer to that as well but heard something
about a fellow called Whyte whose writing had a legal twist.

Then, thank goodness, the door bell rang. Holmes rose
softly and moved his chair toward the door. We heard the servant
pass along the hall, and the sharp click of the door latch.

[handwritten margin note:] De Jure inter Gentes published in Latin at Liège, 1642 Printed by Philippe de Croy. Ex-libris Guilielmi Whyte in faded ink on fly-leaf. Some pragmatic seventeenth-century lawyer.

BABY.—I send something to go on with, which please accept. Will do more if I can. Write me fully, as I don't see how you yourself can arrange. Suppose I get what you want from friends without expense, can it be repaid sometime? Hope you understand. May I ask if it is for yourself. I trust you may consider I am doing my best.

S. E. M.—I should indeed be delighted. Will write now.—March 4th.

3.—Beloved—The top stone was laid with great rejoicing at All Saints, North. Primrose and violets at A. W. E. Much love from Queenie. Five and Nine (E C.)—1, East Bond-street.

10,000£.—NINEMVOONEMVCRTTPFMAPC? WC 61? See many previous advertisements since 31st July, 1879. QFJHCRFT PFHLLM! BSPCFFM? 71? QFJHCRTTFFMMM! I was hated by a pack of tongueless bloodhounds.

FIFTY POUNDS REWARD.—MISSING. HARRIS HILLS, of Stamford-hill, London, a gentleman, aged 38 years, 5 feet 11 inches high, well built; he has rather a downcast look, stooping gait, and shy manner, dark hair, shaved with the exception of small whiskers, dark eyes; dressed in black suit (no overcoat), black woollen gloves, low crowned black hat with mourning band, black scarf necktie, heavy laced-up shoes, three rings on left hand; depressed in his mind. He left his home on Thursday, Feb. 24.

FOUND. In the Brixton Road, this morning, a plain gold wedding-ring found in the roadway between the White Hart Tavern and Holland Grove. Apply Dr. Watson, 221B, Baker Street, between eight and nine this evening.

JEWEL ROBBERY.—TWO HUNDRED POUNDS REWARD will be PAID by Mr. BRYCE WRIGHT, Mineralogist, of 90, Great Russell-street, W.C., on conviction of the thief or thieves, to any person (not being the actual thief) giving such INFORMATION as may lead to the RECOVERY of the JEWELLERY STOLEN from his premises during the evening of the 24th inst.—Particulars of the articles stolen are in the hands of the Police, Pawnbrokers, and Jewellers. Information to be given to Messrs. Beard and Sons, 10, Basinghall-street, E.C.; to the Director of Criminal Investigations, Great Scotland-yard; or to any Police-station.

LOST (TEN SHILLINGS REWARD), a small BUNCH of KEYS, between Lincoln's-inn and Curzonstreet, on evening of 2d March. Whoever brings them to No. 8, Curzon-street, Mayfair, will receive the above reward.

REWARD, £2 10s.—LOST yesterday, supposed on Holborn-viaduct, a GOLD ALBERT FETTER LINK CHAIN, with Oval Bloodstone Seal, Gilt Keys.—Apply to E Nicholls, Porter's Lodge of Ely-place.

MR. JOSEPH STANGERSON, Anyone knowing the whereabouts of the said gentleman, believed to be an American, is requested to contact Mr. Gregson at Scotland Yard, 4, Whitehall Place, or the nearest police station.

TO Mr. D. S. DAVIS, late of 64, Hatton-garden, London.—Unless the LANDAU left by you with me on or about July 15, 1879, is removed, and all charges thereon paid, on or before the 11th inst., the same will be SOLD to defray (as far as possible) expenses.—William Cleave, auctioneer and valuer, 2, Sheet-street, Windsor.

MERCHANT SEAMEN'S ORPHAN ASYLUM.—Mrs KENNEDY desires to THANK all FRIENDS who SUPPORTED the CASE of her SON, ALBERT EDWARD, at the late Election.

NEXT of KIN.—1881 EDITION.—£277,000,000 UNCLAIMED.—A REGISTER containing the names of 41,000 Persons who have been advertised for to claim property and money since 1700. Post free, 2s. 1d.—DOUGAL and Co., 225, Strand.

PRIVATE DETECTIVE and INQUIRY OFFICE for Divorce, missing friends, watching suspected persons, and all private matters.—Mr. COOKE, 16, Delahaystreet, Westminster. London. Female Detectives. Terms 10s. per day.

PRIVATE INQUIRY OFFICE (high-class and old-established).—Mr. WARD, 22, Buckingham-street, Strand, London. Suspected persons watched. Detectives, male or female. Divorce, libel, and confidential cases taken.

TEENS that young ladies are in no hurry to get out of—"LOUIS' VELVET-TEENS."

SPECIAL NOTICE.—PHILLIPS' CHINA and GLASS.—Simply the LARGEST STOCK in LONDON of COMMON and BEST SERVICES of every description, ORNAMENTS, ART POTTERY, and DUPLEX LAMPS DINNER SERVICES from 2s. All GOODS are MARKED in PLAIN FIGURES, the prices presenting opportunities to purchasers not offered by any other house.—W. P. and G. PHILLIPS, 357, 358, and 359, Oxford-street, W.

SPECIAL NOTICE.—BRAND and Co., Original Manufacturers of Essence of Beef (green label) and other Specialities for Invalids. HAVE NOT REMOVED from their sole Address, No. 11, Little Stanhope-street, Mayfair, W.

NOTICE to ADVERTISERS.—SEARBY and Co. are the best PUBLIC COMPANY ADVERTISING AGENTS. Contracts entered into 1881 to 50001.

NOTICE to ADVERTISERS.—SEARBY and Co. are the best TRADERS' ADVERTISING AGENTS. Same rates as papers.

NOTICE to ADVERTISERS.—SEARBY and Co. represent every Newspaper in the United Kingdom. Corrected list supplied free to customers.

NOTICE to ADVERTISERS.—SEARBY and Co. INSERT all LEGAL and NECESSARY NOTICES in the "London Gazette."—Head premises, 1, Queen-street-place, Cannon-street, E.C.

CRYSTAL PALACE.—THIS DAY.—Admission to Palace, ONE SHILLING, or by Season Ticket. Open from 10.0 till 4.30. Tiff's Shiddaw Rock Band, 3.0 and 5.30; Orchestral Concert, 4.0; Great Organ (Mr. A. J. Eyre), 4.30. Skating Rink, 2.0 p.m.

CRYSTAL PALACE.—TO-MORROW, at 3.0, SATURDAY CONCERT.—The PROGRAMME will include Symphony No. 5, in B flat (Schubert); Violin Concerto (Beethoven); Symphonic Poem "Oltava" (Smetana), first time; Fantasia for Violin and Orchestra (Schumann), first time. Vocalist, Mdlle. Orgeni. Solo Violin, Herr Joachim. Conductor, Mr. AUGUST MANNS. Seats, 2s. 6d. and 1s ; admission to Concert Room, 6d.

ALEXANDRA PALACE, TO-MORROW.—CAMELLIA SHOW, by W. PAUL and SON, of Walthamcross. 2000 Blooms will be sold at nominal prices. Play at 4.0, THE DANITES, by Mr. C. H. Morton and Company from Imperial. Promenade Concert at 7.15; Mdlle. Avigliana will Sing "A Shadow" (Cowen), "Woo by a Rose" (Roeckel), and "A Summer Shower" (Marzalls); Mr. Howard Reynolds (Cornet solo). Free seats everywhere. Trains advertised To-morrow.

SACRED HARMONIC SOCIETY, St. James's Hall.—Conductor, Sir MICHAEL COSTA.—This Evening, March 4, at Half-past Seven, Costa's Oratorio, NAAMAN. Principal Vocalists: Miss Robertson, Mrs. Osgood, Madame Patey; Mr Vernon Rigby, Mr. Kenningham, and Mr Santley. Organist, Mr. Willing.—Tickets, 2s. 6d., 5s., 7s., and 10s. 6d., at Society's Office, 7, John-street, Adelphi; Austin's, St. James's Hall; and usual Agents.

COSTA'S "NAAMAN," St. James's Hall, This (Friday) Evening. Miss ROBERTSON, Mrs. Osgood, Madame Patey, Mr. Vernon Rigby, and Mr. Santley. Tickets, 2s. 6d., 5s., 7s., and 10s. 6d. Commence at 7.30.

ROYAL ALBERT HALL CHORAL SOCIETY.—PRESIDENT—H.R.H. the Duke of EDINBURGH, K.G. Conductor, Mr. BARNBY. Under the Special Patronage and in the presence of their Royal Highnesses the Prince and Princess of WALES, Dr. Sullivan's Sacred Musical Drama THE MARTYR OF ANTIOCH will be performed, with the original cast of Soloists, under the direction of the Composer, preceded by Brahm's SONG OF DESTINY, on Thursday Evening, 9th April, at Eight, instead of the 24th March, as announced in the Society's Prospectus. Seats may now be secured. Prices, 10s. 6d., 7s., 5s., 4s., and 1s.

ROYAL AMATEUR ORCHESTRAL SOCIETY.—SMOKING CONCERT.—Conductor, Mr. GEORGE MOUNT—ALTERATION of DATE.—Members and Subscribers are informed that the date of the next Smoking Concert, at St. Andrew's Hall, Newman-street, is unavoidably altered from Thursday, March 17th, to Friday, March 18th, at Nine p.m. J. E. DOW, Hon. Sec.

MR. SIMS REEVES'S LAST BALLAD CONCERT.—St. James's Hall, Tuesday Next, March 8th, at 8.0 o'clock. This is his LAST BALLAD CONCERT in London. Programme:—"Nymphs of the forest," the London Vocal Union; "For ever and for ever," Mr. A. Oswald; "Orpheus with his lute," Miss de Fonblanque; Solo—Pianoforte, "Rhapsodie Hongroise" (No. 8, Liszt), Herr Coenen; "Eveningstar," Mr. Herbert Reeves; "Spanish love song," Madame Trebelli; "Adelaide" (Beethoven), Mr. Sims Reeves; Solo—Violin, "Suite in E" (Bach), Prelude, Minuetto and Gavotte, Herr Joachim, Miss de Fonblanque; Aria "Salve! dimora," (Faust) (Gounod), Mr. Herbert Reeves ; Violin Obbligato, Herr Joachim; Duet, "St. instanchaux" (Trovatore) (Verdi), Madame Trebelli and Mr. Sims Reeves; "The long day closes," the London Vocal Union; Mazurka (Chopin), Madame Trebelli; Solo—Pianoforte, "Valse" (Rubinstein), Herr Coenen; "In this old chair," Mr. Sims Reeves; Solos —Violin, a. "Romance from the Hungarian Concerto" (Joachim), b. "Capriccio" (Paganini), Herr Joachim; Duet, "The moon has raised," Mr. Herbert Reeves and Mr. A. Oswald; Brindisi, "Il Segreto," Lucrezia Borgia (Donizetti), Madame Trebelli; "Cœur de Lion," Mr. A. Oswald; "Robin Adair," Miss de Fonblanque; Song, by desire, "The death of Nelson" (Braham), Mr. Sims Reeves; "The hunt is up," the London Vocal Union. Conductor, Mr. SIDNEY NAYLOR. Tickets—10s. 6d., 7s. 6d., 5s., and 1s.—at Austin's Office, St. James's Hall, and usual Agents.

WEDNESDAY NEXT.—LONDON BALLAD CONCERTS, St. James's Hall, at 8.0 o'clock. Artists :—Miss Mary Davies and Miss Clara Samuell, Madame Antoinette Sterling and Madame Patey; Mr. Edward Lloyd and Mr. Joseph Maas, Signor Foli and Mr. Maybrick; the South London Choral Association of sixty voices, under the direction of Mr. L. C. Venables. Conductor, Mr. SIDNEY NAYLOR. Stalls, 7s. 6d.; area, 4s. and 2s.; balcony, 3s.; gallery and orchestra, 1s. Tickets of Austin, St. James's Hall; the usual agents; and Boosey and Co., 295, Regent-street.

WEDNESDAY NEXT.—The BALLAD CONCERT PROGRAMME will include the following popular Songs:—"She Wandered down the Mountain Side," "What are they to do?" "Spinning," "Duncan Gray," "Robin Adair," "The Chorister," "John O'Grady," "Cassidance" (Cowen), "My Boy Tammie," "Alice, where art thou?" "The Love of long ago" (W. H. Cummings), "Phillis is my only joy," "Love's request, "All in All" (F. H. Cowen), "Maid of Athens" (Allen), "The Pilgrim's Love Song," "St. Mildred's Well" (Louis Diehl), "Gallants of England," "Hearts of Oak," "Two Songs," "You stole my love" (W. Macfarran), "A Spring Song" (Pinsuti), "Choice" (Philip), "Hunting Song (Benedict), "What is Love" (Philp). Bridal Chorus from "The Rose Maiden." Tickets of Booney and Co., 295, Regent-street.

ROYAL POLYTECHNIC.—HUMOROUS MUSICAL SKETCHES, by Mr. Eric Lewis, at 4.0 and 9.0; the Photophone, 2.0; the Lightning Inductorium, 1.0; Astronomy, 7.45; Mr. King; Recitals in Costume, by Madame Katharine Hickson, 3.30 and 7.15; Magic and Mystery, Professor Hellis, 2.45 and 8.30, &c.—Admission 1s. Open 12.0 till 5.0 and 7.0 till 10.0.

MADAME TUSSAUD'S.—The IRISH AGITATION.—Now added, Mr PARNELL, M.P., and Mr. MICHAEL DAVITT; Right Hon. W. E. Gladstone, Earl Granville,

---

PARLIAMENTARY SUMMARY.

In the House of Lords yesterday, Lord LYTTON moved his promised Resolution relating to the declared policy of the Government to abandon Candahar, which he contended was not justified by any information in their Lordships' possession. After reviewing the political situation in Afghanistan prior to the late war, the noble Earl referred to the general feeling among the native Princes of India against the proposed withdrawal of the British forces, and questioned the wisdom of the Government in publishing the minute containing the opinion of military officers on the subject. He also defended himself from the charge of the Duke of Argyll, that he had held the opinions of previous Governor Generals in contempt, and insisted that Russian intrigues had brought about an entirely different state of things from that with which previous Viceroys had to deal. If Candahar were abandoned, and the valley of the Indus made our frontier line, Russia would obtain such an addition of strength at Merv and Herat that nothing short of a general war against her would be sufficient to restore the influence at present possessed by England in Afghanistan. He held that the retention of Candahar would enable the Government to administer our Indian Empire without fear of Afghan treachery or Russian ambition.

Lord ENFIELD expressed his regret that the noble earl had dwelt so long upon the subject of Russian rivalry to this country, and defended the Government from the charge that they had endeavoured to upset all the arrangements of their predecessors in India and in Afghanistan. He adduced evidence of native opinion that British rule in Afghanistan was unpopular, and that any further annexation of territory would be viewed with much disfavour by the native princes of India. Denying that Candahar was a military necessity to India, he argued that in case of hostilities with Russia our forces could operate with advantage from our former frontier, and he quoted the opinions of Sir Henry Rawlinson and others in support of that view. He objected to the retention of Candahar upon the ground of the increase of Indian taxation it would involve, and referred to the conviction of the Afghan people that the object of General Roberts's expedition having been completely attained England would not be justified in retaining a force in their country.

Lord WAVENEY moved an Amendment to the effect that a Commission be appointed to consider and report on the most suitable form of administration for Candahar and its dependencies, advocating its formation into a Crown colony.

Lord CHELMSFORD analysed the military features of the question, stating his belief that India had nothing to fear from a Russian occupation of Afghanistan, and that our troops could successfully contend against any invasion from the Indus.

Lord SANDHURST opposed the Motion, considering the policy of non-intervention the most suitable in the present circumstances.

The Earl of DONOUGHMORE supported the Motion, viewing the proposed withdrawal of the army from Candahar as a national calamity.

The Earl of DERBY contrasted the advantage which might accrue from the retention of Candahar with the bad effect which would be produced by the increased taxation of the people of India. Feeling that our present frontier line offered a sufficient guarantee against invasion, he dwelt upon the difficulties which would meet a Russian force in case of hostile movements. The retention of Candahar would, he thought, be considered as a standing menace upon the part of England, instead of which he advocated a free and strong Government in Afghanistan as the best security against Russian encroachment. He considered that the preponderance of military opinion favoured the retirement of the British troops, and drew attention to the unpopularity

of "Name" were again raised, and the SPEAKER "named" Mr. Healy accordingly, as disregarding the authority of the Chair. Mr. GLADSTONE thereupon moved the usual resolution suspending the hon. member from the service of the House during the remainder of the sitting; and on the question being carried to a division it was agreed to by 233 to 15. Mr. Healy then walked out of the House; and the debate was continued by Mr. T. P. O'Connor, Mr. G. Russell, Mr. Redmond, Mr. Byrne, and Mr. Leamy.

Mr. O'DONNELL indulged in some severe strictures upon the manner in which the Home Secretary was conducting the Bill through the House. It being now a quarter-past nine o'clock,

Mr. CHILDERS moved the adjournment of the debate, to enable him to make his promised statement on army organisation, but here Mr. CHAPLIN interposed with a protest against the encroachment by Ministers on the rights of independent members. Lord HARTINGTON admitted that the House was placed in a novel position, but appealed to the Opposition to remember the understanding that had been arrived at for adjourning the debate at nine o'clock. Lord PERCY too joined in protesting, and Mr. PARNELL contended, in opposition to the adjournment, that if the Arms Bill were urgent the previous day it must be urgent then. When the wrangle had lasted an hour, Colonel STANLEY rose and appealed to the House to consent to the adjournment of the debate in order that Mr. Childers might have an opportunity for his statement at an hour that would be convenient to all parties. Mr. BIGGAR created some merriment by saying that as a general rule his policy was in favour of adjournments. He should therefore vote for the adjournment of the debate in this instance. On the House dividing, the Motion for adjournment was carried by 277 to 28. Then ensued another irregular discussion on questions of order; but after a half-hour thus expended

Mr. CHILDERS was allowed to make his promised statement on the proposed changes in the army. He reviewed the operation of Lord Cardwell's measures of army reform, and pointed out where they had proved defective. After describing the changes to be made in relation to promotion and retirement in the Militia, he said he proposed that for the future the minimum age of recruits should be nineteen instead of eighteen years, the term of service, as now, twelve years, and that the men should serve with the colours for seven years instead of six, and if serving abroad eight years, the rule to be applicable to all arms alike. Papers would be issued to-day giving full particulars as to uniforms, titles, badges, and colours. Under the new system every regiment would take its turn for Indian and colonial service, at much less expense than under the present system. After dealing with the questions of pay, promotion, and retirement, he mentioned that the great blot in the system of regimental promotion and retirement was the great number of compulsory retirements at an early age which would be shortly inevitable. The proposed changes would reduce the number of compulsory retirements, and greatly benefit the officers. Taking the whole of the reforms as applicable to men and officers, India and this country would each in the end gain not much less than 250,000l. a year, while the officer and the soldier would be pecuniarily the better by the average addition to their term of service. It was also proposed to abolish corporal punishment in the army and to substitute a summary punishment in the shape of restraint, without injury to life or limb. Objection might be taken to the present as an inopportune moment for making the proposed changes; but in his opinion the time had come for making alterations which the most able and experienced men believed would add greatly to our military strength and security.

Colonel STANLEY, speaking on behalf of the Opposition, expressed his satisfaction with the

OPINIONS OF THE MORNING PAPERS.

THE RETENTION OF CANDAHAR.

The Standard says Lord Lytton, who on the very first occasion of his addressing the House of Lords, showed that he was a master in the art of catching the ear of the most fastidious Assembly in the world, confirmed this favourable impression last night by the cogency and force with which he brought forward his long-expected motion on the subject of Candahar. The first question that naturally suggests itself in considering this subject is whether Candahar is a place offering in itself any peculiar advantages to induce us to continue our present occupation? The answer given by a number of authorities who, it may be strictly said, were never before arrayed in support of any course of action, is that, as a military position, Candahar is the only place of real importance between the Indus and the Helmund. Nor can it be overlooked that this overwhelming evidence of practical experience and local knowledge is in itself presumptive proof that the retention of Candahar is necessary for the proper administration and defence of the Indian frontier. Lord Derby attempted, but not more satisfactorily, we think, than Lord Enfield, who expressed the official view of the question, to explain away the significance of this agreement of authoritative opinion by asserting that such had always been the case when Anglo-Indian officials were called upon to sanction the incorporation of fresh territory. But this explanation will hardly suffice to deprive the deliberate opinion of such a man as Sir Donald Stewart of the weight it must exercise with all thinking men. The present state of affairs in Afghanistan is an additional reason for hesitating to evacuate this hard-won position. There are two rulers in that country struggling to maintain their places, Abdul Rahman and Ayoob Khan. Neither possesses any solid power. The former lives in daily dread of our old opponent, Mahomed Jan; the latter feels himself so insecure at Herat that, according to telegraphic report, he has sent an envoy to Candahar to solicit our forgiveness of the past, and with a request to place him in command of that city on our departure. Besides these two bitter rivals no other personage remains to whom we can deliver Candahar up; and, as the Government can hardly contemplate abandoning it without leaving some one in authority, it has yet to be stated to whom a city of such importance to ourselves can be safely made over.

The *Morning Post* thinks that whatever may be the diversity of opinion which exists upon the question as to Candahar, there is, at all events, a perfect agreement that whether for weal or for woe the decision of her Majesty's advisers in respect to this question is one of the most important which any Government have been called upon to determine during the past quarter of a century. Before following Lord Lytton in his long but lucid history of Russian intrigue on our North-Western frontier of India, we may take it at all events as a postulate that it is material to the interests of the British Empire that India should be preserved, and that such precautions as would recommend themselves to the prudent statesman should be adopted in order to prevent Russia gaining such a vantage-ground upon our frontier as would endanger the safety of our Indian possessions. But though this postulate was admitted in the course of last night's debate both by the Government and by the Opposition, they differed in what we cannot help feeling was a vital particular as to the means by which this end should be secured. Ought Candahar to be relinquished or retained? Lord Salisbury struck the true keynote when he asked whether, more especially in presence of the recent reverses we have sustained in Southern Africa, we could prudently afford to make such a confession of weakness as would be involved in our abandonment of Candahar. We have to consider not only the prosaic question of what it is at present worth to us, or what it would cost us to retake it a few years hence, when Merv, if not Herat, had fallen into Russian hands, but what would be the impression made upon the millions whom we hold in subjection in India by a confession that we are unable to keep it. Sentiment cannot be thrown out of account, more especially when that sentiment, if misdirected, may lead to disastrous results.

The *Times* says:—The speech delivered yesterday by the Earl of Lytton in support of his motion for the retention of Candahar was at once startling and disappointing. It was disappointing because, though skilfully arranged and eloquently delivered, it added little or nothing substantial to the arguments with which the public is already familiar on behalf of the policy advocated by the late Viceroy. It was startling because it disclosed and avowed a view of frontier policy in India not very likely to be accepted with favour in the future, and very considerably at variance with that avowed in the past by the Government which was responsible for Lord Lytton's acts as Viceroy. Of Lord Lytton's retrospective survey of our relations with Afghanistan down to the autumn of 1878 there is

of non
of prom
maintена
the India
to take t
of linke
the sam
instead
and six i
seven y
reserve.
recruits
they are
confirms
vision, fe
portion o
really yo
age of on
over seve
how Mr.
moment
There wi
general o
of 850,
the batt
will have
to the su
strength
rank and
ments,
1000 b
with th
cavalry,
a state o
indeed.
when c
home, it
spoken o
wars, an
ence had
is a con
Childers
sion mu

TH

No s
in Dubl
League
authorit
There w
the mer
of them
Sunday
the cou
night th
was no
night.

Sir R
Wester
of the
receipt
but the
first ni
on that
mini in
greater
reason o
ticularl
was no
were at
ance co
and agr
as a rea
their c
as bad
an incr
to the
Mr. Fe
Papiste
pany.
to Kno
League
down.
to with
disclai
why we
not giv
Chairm

The
United
or Pa
as life
the Ra
do is
to deb
the pe
not to
that w
in the
attest

THE TUNISIAN QUESTION.

(BY TELEGRAPH.)
(FROM OUR OWN CORRESPONDENT.)
TUNIS (*viâ* Malta), TUESDAY.

Sir Charles Dilke's statements in the House of Commons have created a disagreeable impression here.

The statement that her Majesty's Government have referred the French proposals for the settlement of the Enfida question to the consideration of the law officers of the Crown has caused considerable surprise, following, as it did, on the explicit declaration previously made that both Governments had agreed to leave the matter in the hands of our local tribunal.

The surprise is, perhaps, greatest amongst the supporters of the French cause, who, knowing that the case must go against them if it be decided according to the established local laws affecting real property, had given it up for lost, but now feel their hopes revive at this unexpected turn of affairs.

It will be considered here as a severe blow to the Government of the Bey if the local laws are treated as a dead letter in the disposition of so large a slice of the territory under his Highness's rule.

MYSTERY MURDER IN BRIXTON

In the early hours of this morning a body was discovered at Number 3, Lauriston Gardens, on the Brixton Road. It has been identified as that of Mr. Enoch J. Drebber, an American visitor from Cleveland, Ohio.

Considerable mystery is attached to the case for a number of singular reasons. The Constable who made the discovery was drawn to the house by a lighted candle in the room where the body was found, but the house was known to be unoccupied at the time and no other persons were found on the premises. A quantity of bloodstains lay around the body but there were no signs of a wound nor any signs of the cause of death. No weapon has been found and suicide is not suspected. Money found upon the body had not been touched and the police say that no motive is yet apparent. Letters on the body suggest that the dead man was about to return to America in company with Mr. Joseph Stangerson, for whom the police are now looking with their customary thoroughness.

Scotland Yard has already put two of its most celebrated detectives on the case, Mr. Gregson and Mr. Lestrade. Sources within the Yard confirm that these two men are close colleagues and firm friends, with an enviable record of successful cooperation in a partnership that is an example to their fellow officers. There are rumours that this might prove to be their last case together but the public can have every confidence that they will swiftly bring it to a satisfactory conclusion through their own unaided efforts.

THE METROPOLITAN BOARD.

MEETING THIS DAY.

The usual meeting of this Board was held this morning, at the offices, Spring-gardens, Colonel Sir J. M'GAREL-HOGG, M.P., presiding.

LOANS.—The following recommendations of the finance committee were assented to without discussion :—That the applications of the vestry of Lambeth for permission to borrow 15,000*l.* to defray the cost of paving works, and of the guardians of Marylebone for a loan of 4000*l.* in respect of their schools at Southall and

---

MESSRS. SPILLMAN and YOUNG are instructed to SELL by TENDER a large quantity of English MILITARY, VOLUNTEER, and POLICE UNIFORMS, comprising about 10,000 grey and blue military overcoats and cloaks, 10,000 police and volunteer tunics, 2000 pairs of volunteer and police trousers, 1000 livery coats, 7000 blue and grey capes, saddlery accoutrements, military busbies and helmets, 1000 military jackets &c. Tenders will be received for the whole or part until Wednesday, March 16th.—Forms to be obtained at 5, Bell-yard, Temple-bar, W.C.

THIS DAY'S CITY QUOTATIONS.

(BY SPECIAL WIRE.)
LONDON STOCK EXCHANGE, MARCH 4.

BRITISH GOVERNMENT SECURITIES, &c.
11.6—Consols 99¼ ⅜, Account 99 ⅛ ⅞. New & Reduced 97¼ ⅜ xd, Indian Fours 104¼ 5¼ xd, Three-and-a-half 102 ½ xd 11.7—Metropolitan Board of Works Stock 104¼ 5¼ xd, Liverpool Scrip 100¾ 1¼, Bank of England Stock 291 3

BRITISH RAILWAYS.
Brighton—11.7-136 8
Brighton Deferred—11.0-131 ½, 11.22-130½ 1¼, 11.42-131 ½
11.50-130¼ 1¼, 12.22-130¼ 1, 12.35-130¼ 1¼, 1.2-130¾ 1 1.15-130¼ ½, 1.18-130¼ 1, 1.55-130¼ 1¼, 1.55-131 ½, 2.2-131½ ¼ 2.22-131 ½
Caledonian—11.0-105 ½, 11.21-105¼ ½, 11.22-105¼ ½, 11.31-105¼ ½, 11.50-105¼ ½, 12.20-105¼ ½, 12.47-105¼ ½, 12.51-105 ½, 1.2-104¾ 5¼, 1.6-104¾ 5, 1.13-104¼ ½, 1.33-104¾ 5¼, 1.36-104¼ 5¼, 1.52-104¾ 5, 2.2-104¾ 5¼
Caledonian Deferred—11.7-12 ½
Chatham and Dover—11.0-31¼ 2¼, 1.52-31¼ ⅜
Chatham Pref—11.0-101¼ 2, 11.7-101¼ 2
Gt Eastern—11.2-65¼ ¾, 1.42-66¼ ¾
Great Northern xd—11.7-122 4
Great Northern A xd—11.7-124 ½, 11.41-124 ½, 12.51-123¾ 4¼, 2.26-123¼ 4
Great Western—11.21-125¼ ¾, 11.43-125¼ ½, 12.25-124¼ 5¼, 1.2-124¼ ¾, 1.17-124¼ 5, 2.45-124¼ 5¼
Hull and Barnsley—11.7-132 ½ dis
Lancashire and Yorkshire xd—11.21-131¼ 2¼
Metropolitan—11.7-119¼ ½, 1.33-119¼ ¾
District xd—11.7-73 ¼, 1.33-73 ¼
Midland—11.21-133½ ½, 2.45-133¼ ½
North British—11.2-95¼ ½, 11.15-95¼ ½, 11.20-85¾ 6, 11.30-85¼ ½, 11.40-85 ¼, 11.49-85¼ ¼, 11.43-86¼ ¼, 11.45-85¼ ½, 12.0-86¼ ¼, 12.7-85¼ ½, 12.15-86¼ ½, 12.20-85¼ 6, 12.35-85¼ 6¼, 12.47-85¼ ¼, 1.6-85¼ ½, 1.42-85 ½, 1.52-86¼ ¼
Edinburgh and Glasgow—11.7-334 4¼
North-Eastern x all—11.2-163¼ ½, 11.15-163¼ ½, 11.30-163 ½, 11.40-163¼ ½, 11.49-163¼ ½, 12.7-163¼ ½, 12.20-163¼ ½, 12.47-163¼ ½, 1.38-163¼ ½, 1.6-162¼ ½, 1.15-162¼ ½, 1.33-162¼ ½, 1.42-162¼ ½, 2.0-163 1
North-Eastern New—11.49-56¼ 9
North Staffordshire xd—11.7-81¼ 2¼
North-Western—11.21-158¼ ½, 11.43-158¼ ½, 12.25-157¼ 8¼, 1.2-157¼ 8, 1.17-157¼ ½, 2.0-157¼ 8
Sheffield—11.7-86¼ 7¼, 11.41-86¼ 7¼, 11.42-86¼ 7, 1.52-86¼ 7
Sheffield Def—11.6-49¼ 50¼, 11.30-49¼ 50¼, 11.31-50 ¼, 1.20-49¼ 50, 1.15-49¼ 50, 1.20-49¼ 50, 1.52-49¼ 50¼
South-Eastern—11.7-132 4
South-Eastern Def—11.0-123¼ ½, 11.30-123¼ ½, 11.41-123¼ ½, 11.42-123¼ ½, 11.50-123¼ ½, 1.17-123¼ ½, 1.20-123¼ ½, 1.52-123¼ ½, 2.2-123¼ ½, 2.22-123¼ ½
South-Western xd—11.20-134¼ 5¼

FOREIGN BONDS.
10.57—Egyptian Pref 94¼ 5¼, Unified 71¼ ½, Daira 74¼ 5¼, Peruvian Fives 21¼ ½, Sixes 26¼ ½
11.0—Turkish Fives 13¼ ½, 1869 14 ¼, 1873 13¼ ½
11.1—Spanish Threes 21¼ ½, Twos 40¼ 1
11.12—Russian 1862 91¼ 2¼, 1870 91 ½, 1871 91 ½ xd, 1872 93 ½, 1873 92¼ ½, 1875 84¼ 5¼, Portuguese 51¼ ½
11.22—Hungarian 1871 91 ¼, 1873 90 ½, Gold Rentes 97 ½
French Fives 118 ½ xd, Threes 83 ½, Italian 88¼ ½
11.23—Brazilian 1865 96 7 xd, 1871 96 7, 1875 96¼ 7½
11.24—Turkish 1871 72¼ 3¼, Ottoman Defence Loan 86¼ 7½, Egyptian Pref 94¼ 5¼, Unified 71¼ ½, Daira 74¼ 5¼, Domain 94¼ ½, Spanish Threes 21¼ ½, Mexican 1851 25¼ ½, 1864 13¼ 14
11.27—Japan Nines 108 10, Sevens 109 11, Russian Nicolai 80 1, Charkof-Azof 91 3 xd, Charkow-Krementschug 91 3 xd, Orel-Vitebsk 93 5, Moscow-Jaroslaw 99 101, Anglo-Dutch 96 7, Spanish Land 96 6, Quicksilver 102 4, Turkish 1854 89 91, 1858 20 1, 1862 16 17, Sixes 1865 14 ½, A B C 21¼ 2¼, Austrian Silver Rentes 64¼ 5¼, Paper 63¼ 4¼, Gold 77¼ 8¼, Uruguay 1871 34 5 xd
11.31—Buenos Ayres 1870 91 3, 1873 91 3, Chilian 1866 103 5, 1867 97 9, 1870 87 9, 1873 86 8 xd, 1875 86 8 xd, Chinese 1874-6 106 8, 1877 100 8 xd, Colombian 1873 42 4, Danubian 1864 106 8, 1867 107 9
11.32—Argentine 1868 95 6, 1871 90½ 1½ xd, Dollars 72 3
11.43—Peruvian Fives 21¼ ½, Sixes 26¼ ½, San Domingo 24¼ 5¼, Turkish Fives 13¼ ½, 1869 14 ¼
12.25—Argentine 1868 95 6, 1871 91 2, Dollars 72 3
12.27—Honduras 9 10, San Domingo 24 5
12.28—Chilian 1866 103 5, 1867 97 9, 1870 87 9, 1873 86 8 xd, 1875 86 8 xd, Ecuador 16½ 16¼
12.45—Egyptian Pref 95 ¼, Unified 71¼ ½, Daira 75 ¼
Peruvian Fives 21¼ ¾, Sixes 26½ ¼
12.48—Spanish Threes 21¼ ½, Mexican 1851 25¼ ½
12.49—Turkish Fives 13¼ ½, 1869 14 ¼, 1873 13¼ ½
12.54—Costa Rica Sevens 21¼ ½, Sixes 27¼ 8¼
12.55—Paraguay 14¼ 15¼, Honduras 1870 9 ¼
1.7—Turkish Fives 13¼ ½, 1869 14 ¼, 1873 13¼ ½
1.25—Mexican 1851 25¼ ½
1.42—Peruvian Fives 21¼ ½
2.26—Peruvian Fives 21¼ ¾, Sixes 26 ¼
2.27—Turkish Fives 13¼ ½
2.35—Russian 1862 91¼ 2¼, 1870 91 ½, 1871 91 ½, 1872 93 ½, 1873 92¼ ½, 1875 84¼ 5¼, San Domingo 23 4
2.39—San Domingo 24 5
3.5—Spanish Threes 21¼ ½, Twos 40¼ 1

AMERICAN AND CANADIAN SECURITIES.
10.52—Atlantic First Mortgage New 69¼ 70¼, Second 33 4, Third 16¼ ½, Erie Shares 50¼ 1¼
11.3—Gt Western of Canada 15¼ ⅞s, Grand Trunk 23¼ ½, First Pref 102 ½ xd, Second 47¼ 8¼, Third 47¼ 8¼ xd, Debentures 111¼ 12
11.14—Erie Shares 50¼ 1, Preference 90 2
11.15—United States Funded Fives 103 ¼, 4¼ pc 114¼ ¾ xd, Fours 116¼ 17, Atlantic and Gt Western First Mort New 69¼ 70¼, Second 33 4, Third 16¼ ½, Central of New Jersey Shares 107 10, Consolidated 119 21, Central Pacific Shares 91 3, Erie First Mort 129 31 xd, Fives 99 101, Illinois Central Shares 137½ 8¼, Pennsylvania Shares 68 ¼, Sinking Fund

---

THIS DAY'S SPORTING

GRAND MILITARY AND HOUSEHOLD BRIGADE STEEPLE-CHASES.

SANDOWN PARK, FRIDAY.

The VETERAN STAKES. A Sweepstakes of 5 sovs each, with 100 added; weight for age, with penalties and allowances. About three miles.

Mr. Fletcher's Southdown, by Caractacus—Anna, by Idle Boy, aged, 11st 7lb ... Captain Middleton	1
Lord M. Beresford's Lucy, aged, 12st 3lb ... Owner	2
Mr. L. Tanner's Vibula, 4 yrs. 10st 13lb ... Captain Wardrop	0
Lord Mayo's Merryman, 5 yrs, 11st 3lb ... Owner	0
Mr. J. Scott's Mytton's Maid, b yrs, 12st 4lb ... Mr. Burke	0
Captain Picott's Khedive, aged, 12st 3lb ... Mr. Dalbiac	0
Captain O'Niel's Claymore, b yrs, 11st 3lb ... Captain Smith	0

Betting.—2 to 1 agst Mytton's Maid, 100 to 30 each agst Khedive and Claymore, 7 to 1 each agst Southdown and Lucy. Won by 20 lengths.

HOUSEHOLD BRIGADE HUNTERS' FLAT RACE.

Prophet	1
Nottingham	2
Abelard	3

Four ran.

BETTING ON THE COURSE.
CROYDON HURDLE-RACE.
4 to 1 agst Charles I. (offered.)
11 — 2 — Telegramme (taken.)
LINCOLNSHIRE HANDICAP.
9 to 1 agst Peter (taken.)

MANCHESTER BETTING.
CROYDON INTERNATIONAL.
4 to 1 agst Charles I. (taken.)
4 — 1 — Thornfield (taken.)
7 — 1 — Telegramme (taken.)
LINCOLNSHIRE HANDICAP.
9 to 1 agst Henry George (taken.)
10 — 1 — Peter (taken.)
14 — 1 — Valour (taken.)
16 — 1 — Kaleidoscope (taken.)
20 — 1 — Belfry (offered.)
22 — 1 — Pelleas (taken.)
25 — 1 — Alchemist (taken.)
25 — 1 — Chirper (taken.)
25 — 1 — Deurance (taken.)
30 — 1 — Eminence (taken.)
30 — 1 — Essayes (taken.)
33 — 1 — Early Morn (taken.)
33 — 1 — Post Obit (taken.)
GRAND NATIONAL.
9 to 1 agst Regal (taken.)
10 — 1 — Thornfield (taken.)
11 — 1 — Fairwind (taken.)
12 — 1 — Liberator (taken.)
CITY AND SUBURBAN.
12 to 1 agst Petronel (taken.)

THIS DAY'S COURSING.
SOUTH LANCASHIRE (SOUTHPORT) CHAMPION MEETING.

The SCARISBRICK CHAMPION CUP, for All Ages. Winner, 230*l.*; second, 86*l.*; third and fourth, 30*l.* each; three winners of four courses, 20*l.* each; seven winners of three courses, 10*l.* each; 14 winners of two courses, 4*l.* each.

FIFTH ROUND.
Tory beat Bright Eye | Hector beat Sandy M'Nab
Blackrod beat Tynedale | Artificial ran a bye
SIXTH ROUND.
Tory Boy beat Blackrod | Hector beat Artificial
DECIDING COURSE.
Mr. J. Thornton's bd and w d TORY BOY, by Sterling Boy—Tormentor's Daughter, beat Mr. J. Heaton's w and bk d HECTOR, by Loveapple—Halsall Lass II. (1).
The SOUTHPORT STAKES; winner, 60*l.*; second, 24*l.*; third and fourth, 9*l.* each; four winners of two courses, 4*l.* each.
THIRD ROUND.
Meols Water beat Lady Go- | Gipsy Lad beat Sawney
lightly | Arthur Wellesley beat Maggie
Birtles beat Tantilisation | Lander
FOURTH ROUND.
Meols Water beat Birtles | Gipsy Lad beat Arthur Wellesley
DECIDING COURSE.
Mr. Bentley's GIPSY LAD, by Donald—Ballot Box, beat Mr. Mather's MEOLS WATER, by Lord of Avon—Mary Hill.

THIS DAY'S SHIPPING.

(BY TELEGRAPH.)
ARRIVALS.

GRAVESEND, March 4.—Phoenix, City of Brussels, Wansbeck, Mosse, Antwerp; Concordia, Boulogne; Curfew, Rotterdam; Paulina, Bruges; Pioneer, France; Tar, Ghent.
SAILINGS.
GRAVESEND, March 4.—Iris, Hamburg; Cologne, Nantes, St. Nazaire; Victory, Ghent; Lapwing, Bordeaux; Hamburg, Havre; Neptune, Cette; Jovellonsa, Lisbon; Greece, New York; Olympia, Hamburg; Petrel, Antwerp; Emilie, New York; Blonde, Dunkirk; Trocadero, Calais; Sir R. Peel, Dunkirk.

WRECKS AND CASUALTIES.
(FROM "LLOYD'S LIST.")

Prince, schooner, of Falmouth, Captain Stoden, laden with granite, from Porthleven for London, in taking Rye harbour 3d March, got ashore on the west side of the entrance, and still remains.
Ida, brigantine, of Brevig, Norway, from Charlestown for Harburgh, was in collision with the Partœnia, barquentine, of Liverpool, off St. Catherine's Point on March 2. The Ida is supposed to have foundered; master, mate, and one man saved.
Day Spring, of Dublin for Newcastle, laden with coal for Waterford, struck on Broomhill shoals in Waterford Harbour, and became a total wreck; captain saved by the Duncannon lifeboat; five hands drowned.
Helmi, Russian barque, from Cardiff for Naples, laden with coal, is ashore in Roches Bay, and will become a total wreck; crew, eleven in number, saved, and at Queenstown.
Milford, smack, from Belfast, bound for Mulroy, went ashore off Knockalloo, in Lough Swilly, and will be a total wreck; crew saved.
Pride of Anglesey, schooner, is reported from Tremone

JEWE

Fron
Lucy Jo
time he
and dia
diamond
George
the Plai
in Treg
articles
the art
Lucy Jo
Mr. S
the Pla
fendant
Mr. I
Jury, an
Villa,
Johnson
sents.
a valua
me to g
temper
She tri
leave i
in the
about t
would
see her a
and pas
would b
leaving
her use
skins a
a cost o
50*l.* 12
quarrel
bracelet
frequen
the bra
told he
was too
not me
that sh
possess
trimmin
covered
She cal
we last
the gat
Goody,
pushed
solicito
and Go
—Cross
party.
The
letting
Plain
The I
Plains
morne
This
Mr. I
the Def
The I
Mr. I
mitted
been se
condese
woman
The
stauce
to be s
In th
case ag
order t
served

Yes
intende
Cheshi
ready
was ac
huntin
the aft
White
arrived
Larisco
horses
a furtl
out.
visited
attrac
respec

Our visitor took both of us so completely by surprise that I thought it worthwhile to note down exactly what happened, as near as I can remember. We heard a clear but rather harsh voice ask whether Dr. Watson lived in the house, then the door closed as the maid let our visitor in and someone began to ascend the stairs. The footfall was an uncertain and shuffling one. A look of surprise passed over Holmes's face as he listened to it come slowly along the passage. There was a feeble tap at the door.

I said, come in, and instead of the man of violence whom we had expected, a very old and wrinkled woman hobbled into the apartment. She appeared to be dazzled by the sudden blaze of light, and after dropping a curtsey, she stood blinking at us with her bleared eyes and fumbling in her pocket with nervous shaky fingers. I glanced at Holmes, and his face had assumed such a disconsolate expression that it was all I could do to keep from laughing. The old crone drew out an evening paper, and pointed at our advertisement.

Crone: (curtseying) It's this as has brought me, good gentlemen; a gold wedding-ring in the Brixton Road. It belongs to my girl Sally, as was married only this time twelve-month, which her husband is steward aboard a Union boat, and what he'd say if he come 'ome and found her without her ring is more than I can think, he being short enough at the best o' times, but more especially when he has the drink. If it please you, she

went to the circus last night along with -

    Myself: Is that her ring?

    Crone: The Lord be thanked! Sally will be a glad woman
this night. That's the ring.

    Myself: And what may your address be?

    Crone: 13, Duncan Street, Houndsditch. A weary way from here.

    Holmes: (sharply) The Brixton Road does not lie between
any circus and Houndsditch.

    Crone: (keenly) The gentleman asked me for my address.
Sally lives in lodgings at 3, Mayfield Place, Peckham.

    Holmes: And your name is -

    Crone: My name is Sawyer - hers is Dennis, which Tom Dennis
married her - and a smart, clean lad, too, as long as he's at
sea, and no steward in the company more thought of; but when
on shore, what with the women and what with the liquor shops -

    Myself: (obeying a sign from Holmes) Here is your ring,
Mrs. Sawyer; it clearly belongs to your daughter, and I am glad
to be able to restore it to the rightful owner.

    With many mumbled blessings and protestations of gratitude
the old crone packed it away in her pocket and shuffled off
down the stairs. Holmes rushed into his room and returned
enveloped in an ulster and cravat, saying that she must be an
accomplice and that he was going to follow her and that I should
not wait up for him. (As if I could have slept!) Looking through
the window I could see her walking feebly along the other side,
while her pursuer dogged her some little distance behind.

You thought that my whole theory was incorrect and I thought that I would be led to the heart of the mystery

It was close upon nine when Holmes set out. I had no idea
how long he might be, so I took out my pipe and had another go
at the racy adventures of Henri Murger's <u>Vie de Bohème</u> (I have
been struggling a bit lately but am reaching the better bits
at last). Also wrote up my notebook. Heard the maid and Mrs.
Hudson pass by the door to bed. Holmes did not return till close
on twelve and I knew at once from his face that he had not been
successful. Amusement and chagrin seemed to struggle for the
mastery, until the former suddenly carried the day and he burst
into a hearty laugh, dropped into a chair and said that he
wouldn't have the Scotland Yarders know what had happened for
the world, for he had chaffed them so much himself that they
would never let him hear the end of it.

I could afford to laugh because I knew that I would be even with them in the long run. I don't mind telling a story against myself.

I asked him to explain, which he did. The creature had
gone a little way, he said, when she began to limp and show
every sign of being footsore. She came to a halt, and hailed
a four-wheeler which was passing. He managed to be close to
her so as to hear the address, but he need not have been so
anxious, for she sang it out loud enough to be heard at the
other side of the street: 'Drive to 13, Duncan Street,
Houndsditch', she cried. Thinking that this began to look
genuine, and having seen her safely inside, Holmes perched

Thats an art which every detective should be an expert at.

himself behind. Away they rattled, and never drew rein until
they reached the street in question. Holmes hopped off before
they came to the door and strolled down the street in an easy
lounging way. He saw the cab pull up. The driver jumped down,

and Holmes saw him open the door and stand expectantly. Nothing came out though. When Holmes reached him, he was groping about frantically in the empty cab, and giving vent to the finest assorted collection of oaths that ever Holmes had listened to. There was no sign or trace of his passenger, and Holmes feared it would be some time before he got his fare. On enquiring at Number 13, they found that the house belonged to a respectable paperhanger, named Keswick, and that no one of the name either Sawyer or Dennis had ever been heard of there.

I laughed in amazement to think that the tottering, feeble old woman had been able to get out of the cab while it was in *Old woman* motion, without either Holmes or the driver seeing her, but *be damned!* Holmes replied rather sharply that it was they who were the old women to be so taken in. It must have been a young man, he said, *The get-up* and an active one, too, besides being an incomparable actor. *was inimitable* He had seen that he was followed, no doubt, and used this means of giving Holmes the slip. It showed that the man they were after was not alone but had friends ready to take risks for him.

Holmes then said that I looked 'done-up' and should turn in, so I did, guessing that he wanted to be left on his own to think over the trick that had been played on him. I left him in front of the smouldering fire, and as I sat in bed scribbling out a few notes, I heard the low, melancholy wailings of his violin, and knew that he was still pondering over the strange problem which he had set himself to unravel.

RTED OCCUPATION OF MERV.

[REUTER'S TELEGRAM.]

AY, March 4.—The *Times of India* of to-ishes a telegram from Candahar, stating Russians are either in possession of will be in a few days, in accordance rangements they have made with the iefs.

ETERSBURG, March 4.—The semi-official Russe to-day gives a positive contra-to the telegram from Candahar pub-y the *Times of India*, stating that the s had occupied Merv, in accordance with agement entered into with the Merv The Russian troops, declares the *Agence*, proceeded further than Askabad, and ave received no invitations from the f Merv.

DUKE OF EDINBURGH.

[REUTER'S TELEGRAM.]

, March 4 (Evening).—H.R.H. the Edinburgh arrived here yesterday even-will leave for London in two or three

TH OF PRINCE GEORGE OF HESSE.

[REUTER'S TELEGRAM.]

KFORT, March 4.—Prince George of brother of her Royal Highness the s of Cambridge, died here to-day at the d age of eighty-eight.

EST AMERICAN PRICES.

[REUTER'S TELEGRAM.]

NEW YORK, MARCH 4.

, easy; Stock Market opened firm, but closed Cotton, quiet: Petroleum, steady: Lard, heat, depressed by advices from Europe; xporters doing little: Corn, business chiefly for delivery; Coffee, Sugar, and Iron, unchanged.

	Yesterday's prices.	To-day's prices.
ey, U.S. Government Bonds	4 p.c.	5 p.c.
ey, Other Securities	3 p.c.	3 p.c.
e on London, Sixty Days ...	4.80	4.79½
ransfers	4.82½	4.82
e on Paris	5.25½	5.25
e on Berlin	94½	94⅜
Cent. U.S. Funded Loan	10 ¼	101
d a Half per Cent. ditto ...	111¾	111⅝
Cent. ditto	113⅜	113⅜
Union Telegraph Shares ...	115¼	114½
lroad Shares.........	48	48¼
ond Mortgage Bonds	99¼	99¼
ecy Central Shares	105⅜	10
sey Income Bonds	102	101½
phia and Reading Shares ...	67⅛	66½
acific Shares.........	118¾	122¾
Pacific Shares	87½	8.½
Pacific Bonds.........	112¼	112¾
rk Central Shares.........	147¼	146¼
Shares	132⅛	132
and San Fran. Ordy. Shares	42½	42¼
eferred Shares	65½	64½
ore Shares	120¾	127⅛
and North-West. Pref. Stk.	135	135¼
Southern Shares	81½	82
Day's Receipts at U.S. Ports	17 0 0	24 000
Day's Export to Gt. Britain	4 000	4 000
tto to the Continent	4 000	19 000
Futures (May)	11.47	11.43
Middling Upland	11 7-16	11⅜
m, Crude	7	7
m, Unit. Pipe Line Certf.	85	86
m, Standard White	9¾	9¾
il ox's.........	10¾	10 11-16
ilcox's Futures (April)......	10¾	10 11-16
xtra State Shipping Brands	4.50 4.70	4.55 4.75
d Mixed Western	58	58
Red Winter, on the spot......	1 21	1 22½
Red Winter, del. cur. mth....	1 21	1 21½
elivery next month	1 2 ⅛	1 22
elivery month after	1 21	1 21½
Fair Rio	12 12¼	12 12¼
Good Rio.........	12½ 12¾	12½ 12¾
Fair Santos.........	11½ 12	11½ 12
air Refining Muscovadoes...	7	7
....	8⅛	8⅛
for Grain, sail to Queens- per qr.	4 6	4 6
for Cotton, to Liverpool ...	¼	¼
rtserrie, No. 1 (in yard)	24	24

PHILADELPHIA.

vania Railroad Shares	65¼	65⅛
m, Standard White.........	9½	9½

STATE OF IRELAND.

THE COERCION ACT.

PROCLAMATION OF COUNTIES.

Our Dublin correspondent telegraphed last night: The following proclamation is published to-night in the *Dublin Gazette*:

By the Lord-Lieutenant and Privy Council in Ireland.—Cowper.—We, the Lord Lieutenant-General and General Governor of Ireland, by and with the advice of the Privy Council in Ireland, and by virtue of the Act made and passed in the 44th year of the reign of her Majesty Queen Victoria, intituled "An Act for the better protection of persons and property in Ireland and of every power and authority in this behalf," do by this, our order, specify and declare that the part of Ireland hereafter mentioned—that is to say, the county of Clare—shall, from and after March 5, 1881, be and continue to be a prescribed district within the proclamation, meaning, and conditions of the said Act. Given at Dublin Castle this 4th day of March, 1881. (Signed) Monck, W. E. Forster, Edward Sullivan (Master of the Rolls), S. Woulfe Flanagan, Thomas Steele (Commissioner of Forces in Ireland).

Similar proclamations are issued for ten baronies in the West Riding of the county of Cork, and the whole of the counties of Galway, Kerry, Leitrim, Limerick, Mayo, Roscommon, and Sligo, and the forms of warrants duly given.

According to a telegram received from Cork last night no arrests have yet taken place in the South of Ireland, and, from the generally-accepted opinion, there is a disposition on the part of the Government to proceed cautiously, and not hastily, in the matter. It is not believed the arrests will be of so extensive a character as was at first anticipated.

At a meeting of the Westport branch of the Land League last evening, a resolution was passed regretting the violence of Mr. Dillon's speech in the House of Commons on Thursday.

BRIXTON MYSTERY

SINISTER THREAT TO SOCIETY

The body of Enoch J. Drebber, an American visitor to London, discovered early yesterday morning in an empty house off the Brixton Road, is a sharp reminder of the underlying currents of social disorder that must be kept firmly in check. In the history of crime, there has seldom been a tragedy which presented stranger features. The German name of the victim, the apparent absence of all other motive than revenge, hinted at by a sinister inscription on the wall, both point the finger of suspicion at political refugees and revolutionaries. The Socialists have many branches in America, and the deceased had, no doubt, infringed their unwritten laws, and been tracked down by them.

We are reminded of many dark fears from the past: the *Vehmgericht*, the secret German courts of the Middle Ages; the sinister *aqua tofana* of the Sicilian poisoner Tofana; the notorious Carbonari, the "charcoal burners" of Italy who laid their plots in the dim forests; the disturbing career of the Marchioness de Brinvilliers; the disruptive forces of primitive man inherent in the Darwinian theory; the provocative principles of Malthus, who would have us control population by force, if necessary; the desperate crimes associated with the Ratcliff Highway murders.

The Government should not allow any such insidious forces to break loose in this country. We strongly advocate a closer watch over foreigners in England.

SEVERE SNOWSTORMS AND GALES

A severe snowstorm, accompanied by a gale of unusual violence, has been raging in the North during the past few days. The greatest inconvenience has been experienced by the railways in Scotland. Telegrams of last night state that the London train which left Inverness at twelve noon on Thursday became embedded in snow, the passengers being shut up within the carriages until they were released to-night. The Caithness line is completely blocked, and the Highland Railway is so drifted over that passengers are only booked to Blair Athole (main line). The branches of the Great North of Scotland are practically closed, and on the northern section of the Caledonian one line of rails is only available for both up and down traffic for a considerable distance. The Midland Railway is completely blocked, and the company decline to book through to Scotland. The Scotch express was sent from Carlisle in duplicate. The first portion, containing the Glasgow passengers, got through fairly well, arriving in Sheffield nearly an hour late, but the second portion, containing the Edinburgh passengers, was not so fortunate. After leaving Carlisle it had to encounter the full force of the storm, and on reaching Howes Junction was fairly stopped by wreaths of snow, which rendered all further progress southward impossible.

MONEY MARKET.

FRIDAY EVENING.

As the financial position in the States has now improved, the flow of gold to the Bank of England which the sudden crisis on the other side arrested has been resumed, and a considerable sum, mostly from Holland, went in to-day. Further remittances from abroad are looked for, especially from Paris, where the exchange on London has again risen, and about £300,000 is on the way from Australia, a third of which is due early next week. These satisfactory features of the situation have affected the value of money, and it is now decidedly easier, short loans being obtainable at 2, ¼ per cent., with a downward tendency. The discount demand was quiet and the supply of bills small, so that three months' paper was negotiated at 2½ per cent. In Berlin the open market rate has receded to 1¾ per cent., or 2¼ below the minimum of the Imperial Bank of Germany, which is maintained solely with a view to the prevention of any gold export. The only other incident claiming special mention is the failure of a Darlington Iron Company, announced this morning. It created an unpleasant impression, as indicating that trade in that district has not been so flourishing as was generally supposed—a view which may be confirmed by the Board of Trade figures on Monday next.

On the Stock Exchange the tendency was not so good as yesterday, and English railways were in some cases very dull. The severest fall was in North-Eastern, which was affected by the Darlington failure and the generally less satisfactory advices from the Cleveland district. North British and Caledonian were lower, because the dividend estimates were not so favourable. The utility of the former stock for purposes of speculation may be inferred from the fact that, although the half-year was completed a month since, and its broad results ought to be approximately known, the guesses as to dividend range from 4 per cent. down to *nil*. The stock fluctuated between 86¾ and 84¼, and left off at 85¼, about ½ lower than last evening's price. The Caledonian dividend is not so impenetrable a mystery as that of its neighbour, but the calculation which recently gave 3½ per cent. as the rate of distribution was reduced this morning to 2¾, and the stock suffered in consequence. In the end the loss was only ¼. Of both railways it may be said that the lower the dividend the more likely is it to be considered fairly earned. Brighton "A," which was at the close of business rather firm, was afterwards sold in the street at lower prices on rumours that the Boards had not been able to agree at to-day's conference, and that "war to the knife" would be declared against the South Eastern. American railroads were firm, although not closing at their best, and Canadian were rather dull, Great Western, however, improving a little on rumours that a definite arrangement with the Wabash had been concluded. The latter stock was bought for the same reason.

Foreign Government bonds were offered, especially Turkish, on orders from Constantinople, where it was rumoured that the Sultan had given an unfavourable reply to the Ambassadors on the Greek Question.

Atlantic Telegraph shares receded on the news that the American Court had declined to grant the injunction sought by the Direct Cable company against the consolidation of land telegraph undertakings.

At the Bank about £80,000 in gold was received from the Continent.

The Adriatic has left New York for England with £32,000 in specie.

To-day the silver market was completely disorganised, and, notwithstanding a further fall in prices, no transactions were reported, and the supply by the West India packet was unsold. The nominal quotation for bars was 52⅛d per ounce, showing a fresh decline of ⅛d to ⅛d; but the usual exporters to the East refused to buy, owing to a further reduction in the Indian exchanges, which were wired at 1s 8⅜d. The Hong Kong rate was steady, at 3s 9½d, and the Shanghai at 5s 2½d. Mexican dollars were quoted 51d, being ⅛d lower. Rupee Paper fell ¼, the Four and a Half per Cents. closing at 90½, ¾, and the Four per Cents. at 83¾, 84¼.

A rise occurred on the Berlin and Vienna Bourses, but most securities declined in Paris. The Three per Cent. Rentes, however, improved

prem.; India Four per Cts., 104¾, 105 Three and a Half per Cts., 101¼, 102¼ Four per Ct. Bonds, 16s, 18s prem.; ditto Debentures, 102, 102¼; Bank of Engla 283; Canada Government Intercolonial 109, 111; Metropolitan Board of Work Half per Cts., 104¼, 105¼ ex div.; Corpora Three and a Half per Cts., 1881-3, 9 1884-7, 99, 100; ditto Birmingham Thr per Cts., 98½, 99; ditto Leeds Four per ditto Leicester Four per Cts., 101, 103 pool Three and a Half per Cts., 103¼, 1 chester Four per Cts., 109, 111; ditto Four and a Quarter per Cts., 103¼, 1 Stockton Four and a Quarter per Cts., 1

Colonial Government Securities.—So Five per Cts., 1894-1916, rose 1, to 112, 1

Foreign Government Bonds.—Colom et.: French Three per Cts., ¼; United Cts., ¼; ditto Four and a Half per Cts per Cts., 5-16; Honduras, ½; Aust ditto Gold, Argentine of 1868, and 1873, ½; and Italian of 1861, ½; but F *fall* ½; ditto of 1872, ¼; Turkish Treas 1869, 7-16; ditto of 1873, 5-16; ditto per Cts. of 1865, ½; ditto Defence, ½; and Mexican of 1864, ¼; Egyptian Sta ditto Unified, 3-16; and ditto Prefere Sanieh, ¼. In the following table w comparison between yesterday's and prices. Where no price is inserted yes tions remain unchanged:

STOCKS.	CLOSING Yest.	To-day.	PRICE To-d	
Argentine 6 p.c. 1868 ...	95	95½	95½	
Do. 6 p.c. 1871	91	91½	...	
Do. 6 p.c. (Hard Dol.)	72	72½	...	
Austrian Silver 5 p.c....	65	65½	65½	
Do. Paper 5 p.c.	61½	64	...	
Do. Gold 4 p.c.........	77½	78	77¾	
Brazilian 5 p.c. 1865 ...	95	98	...	
Do. 5 p.c. 1871	96	97	...	
Do. 5 p.c. 1875	95½	97	...	
Do. 4½ p.c. 1879	86	87	...	
Buenos Ayres 6 p.c. 1870	91	93	...	
Do. 6 p.c. 1873	91	93	...	
Chilian 7 p.c. 1866	103	105	...	
Do. 6 p.c. 1867	97	99	...	
Do. 5 p.c. 1870	87	89	...	
Do. 5 p.c. 1873	86	88	...	
Do. 5 p.c. 1875	86	88	...	
Chinese 8 p.c.	106	10	...	
Colombian 4½ p.c.	42	44	43	
Costa Rica 6 p.c. 1871...	27½	28½	...	
Do. 7 p.c. 1872	21½	22½	...	
Danubian 7 p.c. 1864 ...	106	108	102	
Do. 8 p.c. 1867	107	109	...	
Ecuador	15½	16		
Egyptian 5 p.c. Pref. ...	95	95½	95⅛	
Do. 4 p.c. Unified ...	71½	71¾	71½	
Do. Daira San. 5 p.c.	74¼	75	74¾	
Do. State Dom. 5 p.c.	94¼	94¾	94½	
French 3 p.c. Rentes...	82¾	83½	83⅛	
Do. 5 p.c. Rentes......	117¾	118⅛	...	
Greek 5 p.c.	67	70		
Honduras 10 p.c.........	8½	9½	9	
Hungarian 5 p.c. 1871...	90½	91½	...	
Do. 5 p.c. 1873.........	89⅜	89⅞	89⅝	
Do. 6 p.c. Gold Rentes	95¾	96⅝	96⅛	
Italian 5 p.c.........	88½	88⅝	88½	
Do. 5 p.c. Marem. Rl.	88	90	...	
Do. 6 p.c. 1868 Tobacco	100	102	...	
Japanese 9 p.c. 1870......	108	110	...	
Do. 7 p.c. 1873	109	111	...	
Mexican 3 p.c.	25¾	25½	...	
Do. 3 p.c. 1864	13½	14	13½	
Norwegian 4½ p.c. 1878	103	105	...	
Do. 4 p.c.	98	99	...	
Paraguay 8 p.c.	14½	15	...	
Peruvian 6 p.c. 1870 ...	2 ½	26½	25¾	
Do. 5 p.c. 1872.........	21½	21½	21½	
Portuguese 3 p.c.........	51¾	51⅞	...	
Prussian 4 p.c.........	99	100	...	
Russian 4½ p.c. 1850 ...	90	92	...	
Do. 3 p.c. 1859	68	72	...	
Do. 5 p.c. 1862	91½	92	...	
Do. 5 p.c. 1864.........	95	97	...	
Do. 4 p.c. Nicolai Rail.	80½	80½	...	
Do. 5 p.c. 1870 (Railway Loans)	91	91½	...	
Do. 5 p.c. 1871 (Railway Loans)	91½	91¾	...	
Do. 5 p.c. 1872 (Railway Loans)	93½	93¾	...	
Do. 5 p.c. 1873 (Railway Loans)	92¾	92⅞	...	
Do. 4½ p.c. 1875 (Railway Loans)	84½	85	...	
Do. Charkf-Azf. 5 p.c.	91	93	...	
Do. Chrkw-Kts. 5 p.c.	91	93	...	
Do. Moscw-Jar. 5 p.c.	99	101	...	
Do. Orel-Vitebk. 5 p.c.	93	95	...	
San Domingo	23	25	...	
Sardinian 5 p.c.	95	97	...	
Spanish 3 p.c.	21½	21¾	...	
Do. Rio Tinto Bonds	99¾	100¼	...	
Do. Quicksilver 5 p.c.	102	104	...	
Do. Nat. Land 6 p.c....	95	96	...	
Do. 2 p.c. 1877	40¾	41	...	
Swedish 5 p.c. 1868......	103	105	...	
Do. 4½ p.c. 1876	103	105	...	
Do. 4 p.c. 1878	98	100	...	
Turkish 5 p.c. 1854......	89	91	...	
Do. 6 p.c. 1858	20	21	...	
Do. 6 p.c. 1862	16	17	...	
Do. 5 p.c. Gen. Debt..	13½	13¾	12⅞	
Do. 6 p.c. 1865	14	14½	13¾	
Do. 4 p.c. Guaranteed	103	105	...	
Do. 6 p.c. 1869	14	14⅛	13½	
Do. 4½ p.c. 1871	72¾	73	...	
Do. Treasury 9 p.c....	22	22½	21½	
Do. 6 p.c. 1873	13½	13⅝	13¼	
Do. 5 p.c. (Defence)..	86¾	87½	86¾	
U. S. Funded 5 p.c. ...	103¾	103½	103⅝	1
Do. New Fnd. 4½ p.c.	114½	114½	114½	1
Do. 4 p.c.	116¼	116½	117⅛	1
Do. Virginian 6 p.c....	87½	88½	...	
Uruguay 6 p.c. 1871	34	35	...	

THE OXFORD BRIBERY COMMISSION.

STATEMENT BY SIR W. HARCOURT.

The Commissioners yesterday resumed their inquiry, in a Committee-room of the House of Commons, into the alleged corrupt practices at the recent elections at Oxford.

Sir William Harcourt said his connection with Oxford commenced in 1868. His family, however, belonged to Oxfordshire, and his uncle had represented the county since the first Reform Bill. He commenced his political connection with the city as the colleague of Mr. Cardwell. He made a very extensive canvass, and he found then that Oxford was naturally a Liberal constituency. It was in 1872 that he first became aware of the intention to contest the constituency in the Conservative interest. Mr. Hall was chosen as the candidate, and he was a popular man in the city. In 1874 a severe contest was anticipated, but it was not expected that the Liberal majority would be reversed. Mr. Cardwell then obtained a majority of 80, and he himself about double that. He believed that there was a very much larger sum spent on the other side at this 1874 election than had ever been spent before. Certainly it was the first time that Oxford broke out in colours. He remembered that Madeline Tower was covered with blue. He did not think that the Liberals employed colours on that occasion. Mr. Cardwell then went to the House of Lords, and another election took place. He was bound to say that there was extraordinary violence used at that election, and many people were intimidated. People could not go with comfort, hardly with safety, from home. The result of the election was that Mr. Hall was elected by a substantial majority. A large Liberal organisation was started immediately after this. Mr. Chitty was selected by the Liberal Association as a candidate to stand with him. In the first 1880 election he thought the Liberals would have a majority of 400 or 500, and that was founded on examination of the registers. At the first April election forged tickets were issued by the Conservatives to enable a party of men to attend one of the meetings, storm the platform, and put out the gas. The majority obtained by the Liberals at the April election greatly surprised him by its smallness, as he had anticipated at least 400. Then followed the May election, and its history might, he thought, be summed up in a sentence he saw in a paper to the effect that the Conservatives were determined to defeat Sir William Harcourt at any cost. He told the constituency then that there was no expense he would not incur to prevent violence in the town, and to stop fraud and corruption. The Liberals brought Mr Schnadhorst over from Birmingham, and a party of detectives, with that object. He would like to say one word as to the breakfast that was given on the morning of the election. That was given only to men who were to be employed during the day, and who were the pith and bone of the party. He understood it was done in Birmingham. It was not done with a corrupt motive. As to colours he must say he knew very little about them, but he thought they might very well be dispensed with. With reference to the number of persons employed he knew nothing about the details. There were a great many unpaid workers employed. Oxford had always been an extravagant place. He did not think that Oxford was thoroughly corrupt. There was in Oxford, as there were in most places, a residuum of some 300 or 400 men who could be influenced by money. He did not think that Oxford was a place where people would run after money for their votes, but when, as in this case, a large sum of money was brought to bear from outside, the inhabitants were not strong enough to resist the temptation. He desired to bear his testimony to the honesty and integrity of his agents.

By Mr. Cave.—Before contesting Oxford he had made inquiries of Mr. Cardwell as to the probable expense of doing so, and his impression now was that he was told it would cost something like 1200*l.* He went to Oxford in preference to any other place, because Mr. Cardwell informed him that the constituency was a very good and true one. In 1868 he canvassed almost every voter himself, and, with the exception of the man who Prime Minister asserted that trades unions had not been guilty of illegality (hear, hear). Some responsible Minister would one day, with more justice, make the same declaration of the Irish National Land League, who were now to be hunted down out of the way of this reforming Government. Why, where would the Land Question have been but for the action of the Land League? He had seen all of the present Ministry except the Vice President of the Council going into the lobby against the Land Bill of the late Mr. Butt in the last Parliament. The prescience and foresight of the hon. gentleman (Mr. Mundella) ought to have entitled him to a higher position in the Ministry than he occupied (laughter). Quoting Lord Granville during the present session, to the effect that trades unions had committed crime and outrage, he pointed out that his Lordship was in this statement in direct antagonism with the Premier. That policy of attributing all sorts of evil to the agitation for reform was a common one in every movement, and the Land Leaguers had not escaped the usual fate.

POLICE INTELLIGENCE.

BOW-STREET.

Suspected Extensive Frauds.—*Samuel Charles Phillips*, aged 36, of Grosvenor-mansions, Victoria-street, described as a financial agent, was charged, on a warrant before Mr. Vaughan, with obtaining by means of fraudulent pretences one bracket and divers other articles of the value of 160*l.* and upwards with intent to defraud Messrs. James Shoolbred and Co., of Tottenham-court-road.—Mr. J. P. Grain, who prosecuted, said that in all probability there would be several charges made against the Defendant, but at present the proceedings would be confined to two, made by Messrs. Shoolbred and Messrs. Wallace. The Defendant was the son of parents living at Weymouth, and for some years prior to 1876 carried on business in Ely-place, Holborn, as a trimming manufacturer. Last year he was living at 27, Grosvenor-mansions, in handsomely furnished apartments. The furniture belonged to a gentleman who had advertised it for sale. The advertisement was answered by the Defendant, who purchased it, giving bills for the amount of the purchase-money which, however, were never met. Having obtained possession of the furniture, it was alleged that he went to a number of tradesmen in London, to whom he gave orders for large quantities of goods. He invited them to visit, or send some representative to Grosvenor-mansions, where, upon seeing the handsomely-furnished rooms in which he was living, they had confidence in him, and his orders in several cases were executed. In the case of Messrs. Shoolbred and Co., the Defendant had communicated with the firm, and their manager, Mr. Bowen, called on him and received a small order for some Chippendale furniture. Samples were sent, and in the first place an order for 4*l.* 10s. worth of goods was given. This was subsequently increased to 60*l.* or 70*l.* for furniture for Grosvenor-mansions. After that a person calling herself Mrs. Phillips went to Messrs. Shoolbred's, and selected several articles, including a mantle, value 30*l.*, and a costume, value 31*l.* 10s.; the whole amounting to nearly 100*l.* In November she went again, and referred to what she had purchased before, and gave an order for 60*l.* worth of underclothing. The result was that, for the first time, a communication was made to Mr. Bowen, who instituted inquiries, and found that goods had been delivered to Phillips to the extent of 161*l.* Finding that no arrangement had been made for credit he refused to allow the last goods ordered to be delivered, and immediately communicated with the firm's solicitors, who wrote to the Defendant, demanding payment of 161*l.* He admitted having had all the goods ordered by himself and Mrs. Phillips, but said it was absurd to ask for payment, as he had arranged for credit for six months. A reply stated that no such arrangement had been made, as the invoices would show that the goods were to be sold for cash. Proceedings were taken against him, and he filed an affidavit, in which he swore that he had arranged for credit. The case was adjourned, and subsequently an order was made against the Defendant without, however, a satisfactory result. Four bills of sale for 100*l.*, 275*l.*, 225*l.*, and 250*l.*, had been given. Upon this becoming known an information, embodying all the facts mentioned, was drawn up, and a warrant was granted for the Defendant's arrest. A second warrant was also applied for against him on the charge of perjury.—After some evidence had been given in support of the charge, the Defendant was remanded.

BRIXTON MYSTERY

LAWLESS OUTRAGE

The public will recognize, in the murder of Enoch J. Drebber, in an empty house off the Brixton Road, early yesterday morning, another of those lawless outrages that we have sadly come to expect under a Liberal Administration. Such atrocities arise from the unsettling of the minds of the masses, and the consequent weakening of all authority.

The deceased was an American gentleman, who had been residing for some weeks in the Metropolis, where he had been staying at the boarding-house of Madame Charpentier, in Torquay Terrace, Camberwell. He was accompanied in his travels by his private secretary, Mr. Joseph Stangerson. The two bade adieu to their landlady upon Tuesday, the 4th inst., and departed to Euston Station with the avowed intention of catching the Liverpool express. They were afterwards seen together upon the platform. Nothing more is known of them until Mr. Drebber's body was discovered, many miles from Euston. How he came there, or how he met his fate, are questions which are still involved in mystery. Nothing is known of the whereabouts of the man Stangerson.

We are glad to learn that Mr. Lestrade and Mr. Gregson, of Scotland Yard, are both engaged upon the case, and it is confidently anticipated that these well-known officers will speedily throw light upon the matter.

GREENWICH.

CHARGE OF FORGERY AND THEFT.—*John Wickham* [illegible]

SPORTING INTELLIGENCE

GRAND MILITARY AND HOUSEHOLD BRIGADE (SANDOWN PARK) STEEPLE-CHASES—FRIDAY.

(FROM OUR OWN CORRESPONDENT.)

The VETERAN STAKES. A Sweepstakes of 5 sovs each, with 100 added; weight for age, with penalties and allowances. About three miles.

Mr. Fletcher's Southdown, by Caractacus—Anna, by Idle Boy, aged, 11st 7lb .... Captain Middleton 1
Lord M. Beresford's Lucy, aged, 12st 3lb .... Owner 2
Mr. L. Tanner's Vibula, 4 yrs, 10st 3lb .. Captain Wardrop 0
Lord Mayo's Merryman, 5 yrs, 11st 3lb .... Owner 0
Mr. J. Scott's Mytton's Maid, 5 yrs, 12st 4lb.... Mr. Burke 0
Captain Pigott's Khedive, aged, 12st 3lb...... Mr. Dalbiac 0
Captain O'Niel's Claymore, 5 yrs, 11st 3lb.. Captain Smith 0

Betting.—2 to 1 agst Mytton's Maid, 100 to 30 each agst Khedive and Claymore, 7 to 1 each agst Southdown and Lucy. Merryman refused the first obstacle, after clearing which Southdown drew clear of Vibula and Khedive, but at the end of half a mile Southdown dropped back, leaving Vibula in command. Passing the stand, Southdown resumed the lead, with Vibula next to the bottom of the hill. Here the last-named came to grief, as did the favourite at the fence past the water jump, and the field being further reduced by the falling of Khedive and Claymore at the last fence but one, Southdown was left with a long lead, which he held to the end, and won easily by 20 lengths from Lucy. Nothing else passed the post.

The HOUSEHOLD BRIGADE HUNTERS' FLAT-RACE PLATE of 150 sovs for the winner, and 30 sovs for the second; 12st each, winners extra; allowances. About two miles on the flat.

Colonel Harford's (Scots Guards) Prophet, by Solon—Lyra, aged, 11st .... Hon. L. White 1
Mr. W. G. Craven's (late 1st Life Guards) Nottingham, 5 yrs, 12st 7lb...................... Lord D. Gordon 2
Colonel Sharp's (late Scots Guards) Abelard, aged, 12st 7lb Owner 3
Mr. A. C. Jervoise's (late Coldstream Guards) Cherry Pie, 5 yrs, 11st 7lb .... Mr. Brocklehurst 0

Betting.—11 to 10 on Nottingham, 5 to 4 agst Prophet, 25 to 1 agst any other (offered). Prophet made all the running, and won by ten lengths; bad third.

The LIGHT-WEIGHT GRAND MILITARY SWEEPSTAKES of 10 sovs each, h ft, with 150 added; 11st each; winners extra; second horse to save stake. Grand Military Gold Cup Course.

Major Murray's (3d Dragoon Guards) Beaufort, by Lord Ronald—Breda, 5 yrs, 11st 7lb.......... Mr. Lee Barber 1
Mr. Doyne's (13th Hussars) Hawkeye, 5 yrs, 11st 7lb Owner 2
Mr. R. J. Abdy's (4th Dragoon Guards) Emily, 6 yrs, 11st 7lb Mr. L. H. Jones 3
Mr. H. S. Dalbiac's (R. H. A.) Herzegovina, 5 yrs, 11st Owner 0

Betting.—Evens on Beaufort, 2 to 1 agst Hawkeye, 5 to 1 agst Herzegovina. Emily cut out the work attended by Hawkeye, with Herzegovina last to the top turn, where Hawkeye took the lead. At the water-jump, Herzegovina refused, and Beaufort, heading Hawkeye at the last jump, where the latter's jockey broke a stirrup-leather, won by three lengths; a length between the second and third.

The SANDOWN MILITARY and OPEN HUNTERS' SELLING PLATE of 80 sovs; weight for age, with selling allowances. Two miles and a half, on the flat.

Mr. A F. Peyton's Evenley, by Make Haste—Nisidia, aged, 12st 2lb (50*l.*)............................ Owner 1
Captain Paget's Woodcock, aged, 12st 2lb (50*l.*) Lord M. Beresford 2
Mr. G. Lambton's Burgomaster, aged, 12st 2lb (50*l.*) Owner 3
Mr. A. F. Peyton's Quickstep, aged, 12st 2lb (50*l.*) Mr. Gore 0
Mr. F. A. Garden's Starveall, 5 yrs, 11st 10lb (50*l.*) Captain Smith 0
Mr. D. V. Pirie's Valentine, 4 yrs, 11st 7lb (100*l.*) .. Owner 0
Sir W. Throckmorton's Pennon, 5 yrs, 12st 10lb Mr. Crawshaw 0

Betting.—11 to 8 on Pennon, 5 to 1 agst Evenley, 6 to 1 agst Burgomaster, 10 to 1 Woodcock. Quickstep, Pennon, and Evenley, alternately held the lead for the first half mile, and than Woodcock took a decided lead, but on enteriег the straight Evenley pulled himself to the front, and making the remainder of the running, won in a common canter by five lengths; bad third. The winner was bought in for 200 guineas.

The GRAND MILITARY HUNTERS' STEEPLECHASE of 5 sovs each; weight for age; winners extra. Three miles.

Mr. R. B. Firman's (23d Regt.) Mickey, by Roman Bee—Dagmar, 5 yrs, 12st 1lb .... Mr. La Terriere 1
Lord Torphichen's (Rifle Brigade) Gramont, 5 yrs, 11st 8lb Mr. Lee Barber 2
Mr. Wickham's (R.H.G.), Sober Boy, 5 yrs, 12st 8lb Owner 3
Mr. F. Waldron's (R.H.A.), Lady Mary II., 6 yrs, 12st 10lb Mr. Little 0
Mr. L. H. Jones's (6th Lancers), The Mallard (h b), aged 12st 3lb .... Owner 0
Mr. W. Hayhurst's (Royal Fusiliers), Priesthood, 6 yrs, 12st 3lb...................................... Mr. Purcell 0

Betting.—5 to 2 agst Sober Boy, 3 to 1 agst Gramont, 7 to 2 agst Mickey. The last named got off in front, was never caught, and won in a canter by four lengths; bad third.

One expects a newspaper to get its dates correct! Tuesday was not the 4th

[illegible] 3
[illegible] Owner 0
[illegible] agst Sloth, 100 to 30 [illegible] Admington made [illegible] the stand the last time, [illegible] ten lengths; bad third.
[illegible] STEEPLECHASE PLATE was declared void.

[illegible] BETTING ON THE COURSE.

CROYDON HURDLE-RACE.

4 to 1agst Charles I. (o.)	11 to 1agst Thornfield (t.; after 4 to 1 laid)
11 — 2 — Telegramme (t.)	8 — 1 — Venice (o.)

LINCOLNSHIRE HANDICAP.

9 to 1agst Peter (t.)	25 to 1agst Kuhlshorn (t.)
9 — 1 — Henry George (o.)	30 — 1 — Early Morn (t.)
100 — 7 — Valour (t.)	

BETTING IN LONDON [illegible]

OXFORD ELECTION COMMISSION.

STATEMENT BY THE HOME SECRETARY.

Yesterday the Oxford Election Commissioners —Mr. Cave, Q.C., Mr. Cowie, and Mr. Edward Ridley —again sat in a Committee Room of the House of Commons, and took further evidence.—Sir William Harcourt, with the permission of the Chief Commissioner, made a statement as to his political connection with the borough of Oxford. His connection with Oxford, he said, began in 1868. It was a natural connection. His family belonged to that county, and his uncle was a representative of it since the first Reform Bill. He began as a colleague of Mr. Cardwell, which he always regarded as a great advantage. He believed that very much more money was spent on the first election of 1874 than had ever been spent before. Shortly after the election of 1874 the Liberals determined to retrieve their position, and they established an association with large numbers of volunteer workers, the results of which were seen in the municipal contests in the North Wall. They displaced the two Conservatives there with Mr. Buckle and Mr. Cooper. At that moment it was quite plain that the tide had turned in favour of the Liberal party. That would be either in 1877 or 1878. It was for the Liberal Association to choose their own candidate; in fact, they had established themselves to do away with the old system of wire-pulling, and allow the Liberal constituency a voice in the choice of their candidate. Mr. Chitty was selected, and he came forward. Mr. Chitty asked him the probable cost of the election, and he said it would probably cost them about 1,500l. or 2,000l. each. He suggested that they might make it less, but elections were very much like wars—one party firing off handbills, and the other answering them. However, that was his impression at the time. So things stood until the beginning of 1880. They went down, knowing the election could not be very far off, and after going carefully through the canvass books the result to his mind then was that they should have a majority of 300, 400, or 500. His calculation was always formed on a deduction of 20 per cent. upon the promises. The books were made for the very purpose of being gone through: the moment a dissolution took place the people could go round and verify them. Then came the dissolution, and he wished to say, if he were questioned upon it, that the popular sentiment was as much in favour of the Liberal party in 1880 as it had been adverse to them in 1874. That was the general feeling, and it satisfied him of the truth of an expression which Mr. Cardwell made on a previous occasion, that Oxford was a good political barometer. He anticipated that without doubt their majority at that election would be 400 or 500, and that he should have a little more than Mr. Chitty, as Mr. Cardwell had had more than he, being the older member. Of course they were at a disadvantage never having a committee room in a public-house. Of course the public-houses were all against them. Well, the first election of 1880 was fought very much after the fashion of that of 1874, and it cost very near the sum he had put down, though it might seem an extravagant one— 3,000l. One matter to which he must refer was that of the forged ticket. The tone of Oxford was so changed that they were obliged to give admission to their meetings by ticket to prevent disturbance. In the middle of the first election the other side printed tickets in imitation of the Liberal tickets. A man of the opposite party asked a cabman to distribute them, stating that it was the intention to break up the meeting, put out the gas, and storm the platform. He determined that the constituents should not be overawed, and caused magisterial proceedings to be taken. When he went to Mr. Hall—and he was bound to acquit Mr. Hall of any complicity in the transaction—he declared his intention to put a stop to it. At the meeting between 50 and 60 of these forged tickets were detected in the hands of people, and he supposed they had not been able to call them all in. Mr. Chitty and he put forth a public protest against such conduct, but he was sure Mr. Hall had no cognisance whatever of the matter. It was an attempt by force and fraud to overawe the expression of the constituents, and he was determined at that election and elections afterwards to take all measures necessary to prevent such a transaction as that. That was all he had to say with reference to the first election except as to the result. It ended, as they knew, in his having a majority of 100, and Mr. Chitty about 10, instead of 400, as he had believed. He took office, and went down, he remembered, to Oxford from Windsor, just after he had been sworn in, and he then heard there was to be a contest. It was mooted all about the place that 3,000l. had come down from London from the Carlton. He confessed the moment he heard that he told his friends that he believed 3,000l. would bring an influence to bear on the constituency which it would be almost impossible to resist. He was bound to say in defence of Oxford that he believed that contest was forced upon Oxford from outside. He did not believe it was the desire of the Conservative party or of Mr. Hall. That was his own impression. In one sentence, as uttered by Mr. Perceval Walsh before the Commissioners, the contest was to defeat Sir W. Harcourt. It was on that footing that the contest was fought. Just introduced to a laborious office, he was not able to pay that personal attention to the second election of 1880 which he had done to the former but

IRELAND.

PROCLAMATIONS UNDER THE COERCION ACT.

(BY TELEGRAPH.)

(FROM OUR OWN CORRESPONDENT.)

DUBLIN, FRIDAY NIGHT.

Proclamations by the Lord-Lieutenant and Privy Council in Ireland are published in to-night's *Gazette* declaring that from and after to-morrow the county of Clare, ten baronies in the county of Cork, and the whole of the counties of Galway, Kerry, Leitrim, Limerick, Mayo, Roscommon, and Sligo, be and continue to be described districts within the meaning of the "Act for the better Protection of Persons and Property in Ireland." The forms of warrants under which arrests are to be made are appended to the proclamations.

The Chief Secretary for Ireland was at the Castle unusually early this morning, and on his arrival Mr. Forster was met by the Under-Secretary for Ireland and the Hon. Charles Bourke, chairman of the Prisons Board. Later on, in pursuance of arrangements previously made, the resident magistrates from the various disturbed counties in Ireland attended, and laid before the Chief Secretary the information at their disposal in reference to the condition of their respective districts, and the working of the Act, and the state of crime.

Mr. Dillon's speech has caused considerable excitement. The *Freeman's Journal* makes allowance for the provocation which it says Mr. Dillon received from the Home Secretary, whose recent speeches, it says, "were enough to exasperate a man of a more phlegmatic nature than Mr. John Dillon"; but "this," it says, "cannot justify the language Mr. Dillon used." It says: "We deeply deplore the speech delivered by Mr. Dillon, both because of the nature of the speech itself and its effect in England, as well as its possible effect in Ireland. There is not a single man connected with the Land League for whom, because of his earnestness and honesty of purpose, we have greater respect than Mr. Dillon:

BRIXTON MYSTERY

POLITICAL REVENGE

Early yesterday morning, the body of Enoch J. Drebber, of Cleveland, Ohio, was discovered by the police in an empty house off the Brixton Road. The motive for his murder is thought to be revenge and the police are looking for Mr. Joseph Stangerson, believed to be Mr. Drebber's secretary, whom it is thought will be able to throw some light on the mystery.

There is no doubt as to the crime being a political one. The despotism and hatred of Liberalism which animates the Continental Governments has had the effect of driving to our shores a number of men who might have made excellent citizens were they not soured by the recollection of all that they have undergone. Among these men there is a stringent code of honour, any infringement of which is punished by death.

Every effort should be made to find the secretary, Stangerson, and to ascertain some particulars of the habits of the deceased. A great step has been gained by the discovery of the address of the house at which he boarded – a result which is entirely due to the acuteness and energy of Mr. Gregson of Scotland Yard.

SEVERE GALE AND SNOW STORMS.—The severe gale and snow storms which have been experienced in the North, continued in many places yesterday. Snow fell heavily for several hours in Sheffield yesterday, and in some of the streets it lay so deep that traffic was greatly impeded. Between Sheffield and Manchester the snowfall was very heavy, and the line was blocked with deep drifts at Hadfield. Both the 10.20 and 11.11 trains from Manchester to Sheffield got through with difficulty. The snow plough had to be used, and the trains were two hours late at Sheffield. An engine got off the line at Silkstone in consequence of the snow, and another engine got off the rails at Nostel Priory. A large vessel has been lost yesterday, with all hands, off Souter Point Light. At low water the masts and spars of the vessel washed ashore, and subsequently a boat having painted on it the words, "Cecilia, of Liverpool," together with a figurehead representing a lady, painted white. A vessel named the Cecilia, of Liverpool, left Shields on Thursday. The brigantine Dayspring, of Dublin, bound from Newcastle for Waterford with a cargo of coal, struck on the Broomhill shoals in Waterford Harbour, and became a total wreck.

Money weaker.
Wheat delivery.
The wheat ports have 4,641,065 bales; and total since ports, 865
Call Money
Call Money
Exch. on I
Cable Tra
Exchange
Exchange
Five p. Ct.
Four-and
United
Four p. C
Western R
Erie Rail
Erie Secor
New Jers
New Jers
Philadel.
Union Pa
Central P
Central P
New York
Illinois Sh
St. Louis &
St. Louis &
Lake Shor
Chicago &
Canada S
Cotton,
United
Cotton,
Great F
Cotton, D
Cotton, M
Cotton, N
Petroleum
Petroleum
Petroleum
Lard, Wi
Lard, W
April &
Flour, Ex
Corn, old
Wheat, N
Wheat, N
Wheat, R
Wheat, R
Coffee, F
Coffee, G
Coffee, F
Sugar, Fa
Saltings.
Freight
Queens
Freight fo
pool
Iron Gart

Pennsylva
Petroleum

Cotton, M

GE

DEATH

Prince of
ness the F

GUILDFORD, KINGSTON, and LONDON RAILWAY.—PETITION FOR ADDITIONAL PROVISION.—(Deviation of Railway No. 15 by Wimbledon Common and Putney Heath.)

NOTICE IS HEREBY GIVEN, that APPLICATION is intended to be forthwith made to PARLIAMENT for leave to amend the provisions of the BILL now pending in the House of Commons under the above short title, and to authorise a deviation in the line and levels of the Railway therein referred to as No. 15, as shown upon the plans and sections of the undertaking deposited with the clerks of the peace for the counties of Surrey and Middlesex respectively in the month of November last, which proposed deviation will be wholly situate in the county of Surrey, and in the parishes of Kingston-upon-Thames, Wimbledon, Putney, and Wandsworth, or some of them, and will commence in the parish of Wimbledon, near Coombe Bridge, in a field numbered 1 in that parish on the said plans, and on the eastern side of the stream known as Beverley Brook, at a point on the centre line of Railway delineated thereon, in the fourth mile, at a distance of 8¼ chains or thereabouts from the commencement of the fourth mile from the commencement of the said Railway No. 15, and will terminate in the parish of Wandsworth, near the point where the Kingston-road enters the east side of Putney-heath, on the western side of the road numbered 4 in that parish on the said plans, near the termination of the sixth mile of the said Railway, as marked upon the said centre line, and it is proposed to confer upon the Company to be incorporated by the Bill powers for the purchase by compulsion or agreement, for the purposes of the said deviation, of lands or easements over or under and through lands including one acre or thereabouts between the limits of lateral deviation defined upon the plans hereinafter referred to of the land adjoining Beverley Brook known as Beverley-lane, and being or reputed to be part of Wimbledon Common or Putney Heath, in the parish of Putney, no part of which will be required to be taken, but only an easement over ten perches or thereabouts, to carry the Railway by means of a bridge over the said lane, without touching or interfering with the surface thereof, and also including 36 acres or thereabouts within the said limits of deviation of Putney-heath, in the parishes of Putney or Wandsworth, or one of them, but of which no part of the surface will be required to be taken, but five acres of the subsoil, or an easement therethrough, for constructing a tunnel, and to enact that it shall not be lawful for the said Company to construct any work upon, or take or purchase any part of Wimbledon Common, in the parish of Wimbledon, or to construct any work upon the surface of Putney Heath, or to construct the Railway in, through, or over any part of Putney Heath, otherwise than in tunnel and by the bridge as aforesaid, and within the said limits of deviation, or to take or purchase any part of the surface of Putney Heath, except that not more than five acres or thereabouts of the subsoil thereof, or an easement therethrough, for the construction of the said tunnel. And it is proposed to vary or extinguish all rights and privileges in, over, or connected with the lands proposed to be taken for the purposes of the said deviation, and to confer other rights and privileges, and to authorise the levying of tolls, rates, and charges in respect of the said deviation.

And Notice is Hereby also Given, that plans and sections of the proposed deviation, and books of reference to the said plans, containing the names of the owners and lessees, or reputed owners and lessees, and of the occupiers of the lands which may be taken for the purposes thereof, have been or will, on or before the 12th day of March, 1881, be deposited for public inspection with the Clerks of the Peace for the counties of Middlesex and Surrey respectively, and that copies of so much of the said plans, sections, and books of reference as relate to the parishes of Putney and Wandsworth have been or will, on or before the same 12th day of March, be deposited with the Clerk of the Wandsworth District Board of Works, at his office at Battersea-rise; and as relates to any other parish, have been or will, on or before the same 12th day of March, be deposited with the parish clerk of each parish, at his residence, and that each such deposit will be accompanied by a copy of this notice.

Dated the 5th day of March, 1881.
BURCHELLS,
5, Broad Sanctuary, Westminster;
JAMES BELL,
Kingston-upon-Thames;
HART HART and MARTEN,
Dorking,
Solicitors for the Bill.
SHERWOOD and Co.,
7, Great George-street, Westminster,
Parliamentary Agents.

THREE PER CENT. METROPOLITAN CONSOLIDATED STOCK. Interest payable quarterly.—First Issue £2,450,000 (authorised by her Majesty's Treasury under Act 32 and 33 Vic., cap. 102, and the Acts extending or amending the same). Minimum Price of Issue £90 per cent.; First Dividend Payable on 1st August, 1881.

Special attention is invited to the following clause of the Metropolitan Board of Works Loans Act of 1871:—

"A trustee, executor, or other person empowered to invest money in public stocks or funds or other Government securities may, unless forbidden by the will or other instrument under which he acts, whether prior in date to this Act or not, invest the same in Consolidated Stock."

The Metropolitan Board of Works GIVE NOTICE that they will be prepared to receive, on the 11th instant, at the Bank of England, sealed TENDERS for £2,450,000 of THREE PER CENT. METROPOLITAN CONSOLIDATED STOCK. The money is required for street improvements, artisans' dwellings, main drainage extension, fire brigade stations and plant, and other new works; also for loans to the School Board for London, the managers of the Metropolitan Asylum District, vestries, district boards, guardians, and such other metropolitan bodies as are empowered, by statute, to borrow from the Metropolitan Board.

This stock will bear interest at the rate of £3 per cent. per annum, payable quarterly, at the Bank of England (dividend warrants being transmitted by post, if desired), on 1st February, 1st May, 1st August, and 1st November; and it will be redeemed at par on the 1st February, 1941, should the same not have been previously cancelled by purchase in the open market under the operation of the Redemption Fund constituted by the principal Act.

The books of the Three per Cent. Metropolitan Consolidated Stock will be kept at the Bank of England, where all assignments and transfers will be made, and holders of the stock will be able to take out stock certificates, transferable to bearer, with coupons attached, at the same rate of charge as in Government Stock, if they so desire.

All transfers and stock certificates will be free of stamp-duty.

The security for this stock is the same as for the Three-and-a-Half per Cent. Stock already created, and rests, primarily, on the power of the Board to rate the whole rateable property within the Metropolitan area, as defined by the Metropolis Local Management Act of 1855. The annual rateable value of this area, which will come in force on the 6th April next, amounts to £27,400,000, and a rate of one penny in the pound will produce upwards of £114,000. The Board's debt now outstanding is practically the same as it was on the 1st of January, 1881, when it stood as follows:—Three-and-a-half per Cent. Consolidated stock, £16,984,226; and liabilities, £1,942,513; total, £18,926,889; but on the other hand the Board had assets in loans advanced to other Metropolitan bodies of £3,345,264, and surplus land and property estimated at £2,988,105. The net liability on account of debt was, therefore, £12,593,490.

Under the above statutes a special fund has been constituted for paying the dividends on, and redeeming the principal of, all Metropolitan Consolidated Stock; and the Lords Commissioners of her Majesty's Treasury control the sum to be raised annually by the consolidated rate to meet the charges on this fund.

THE SUNDAY EVENING ASSOCIATION to bring together all persons who, estimating highly the elevating influence of music, the sister arts, literature and science, desire, by means of meetings on Sunday Evenings, to see them more fully identified with the religious life of the people.—Neumeyer Hall, Hart-street, Bloomsbury, TO-MORROW (Sunday), EXHIBITION of MICROSCOPES, &c. From 7.30 to 10 o'clock. Admission free. An annual subscription of half-a-crown constitutes membership.
REUTER E. ROTH, 48, Wimpole-street, W.

ARGYLE-SQUARE CHURCH, King's Cross. LECTURE TO-MORROW EVENING, by the Rev. JOHN PRESLAND, "Religion in its Relation to Life—Death the Gate of Life."—Service at 7 o'clock. The public are respectfully invited.

LLOYD HARRIS will PREACH at Church of the Pilgrim Fathers, opposite Paragon, New Kent-road, TO-MORROW, 11 a.m., "The Crown of Life," 6.30 p.m., "Certain Strange Things." A cordial welcome to everybody.

SCOTTISH NATIONAL CHURCH, Crown-court, Russell-street, Covent-garden. The Rev. ROBERT MILNE, of the Abbey Church, Edinburgh, will PREACH TO-MORROW MORNING at 11; EVENING, 6.30.

STAMFORD-STREET CHAPEL (Unitarian), Blackfriars-road.—The Rev. W. COPELAND BOWIE will PREACH on behalf of the CHARITY ORGANISATION SOCIETY TO-MORROW MORNING, March 6. A collection will be taken in aid of the St. Saviour's (Southwark) branch of the Society.—Service commences at 11 a.m.

ITALIAN CHURCH, Hatton Garden, E.C.—TO-MORROW, being the first Sunday in March, GRAND SERVICE in the Evening at 7.

THE REV. CHARLES VOYSEY will PREACH at the Service of The Theistic Church, held at Langham-hall, 43, Great Portland-street, W., TO-MORROW MORNING, at 11.15. All seats free except those reserved for regular seat-holders.

THE REV. JOHN MONRO GIBSON, D.D., will PREACH in St. John's Wood Presbyterian Church, Marlborough-place, TO-MORROW (Sunday, Morning at 11, and evening at 7. Subject in the evening—"The Sabbatical Year and the Jubilee," in completion of Lectures on Leviticus.

UNITARIAN AFFIRMATIONS.—The following DISCOURSES on "The Positive Aspects of Unitarian Thought and Doctrine" will be delivered, under the direction of the British and Foreign Unitarian Association, in St. George's Hall, Langham-place, London, in March and April, 1881:—
TUESDAY, March 8.—"The Affirmation of God," by the Rev. R. A. ARMSTRONG, B.A.
FRIDAY, March 11.—"Worship and Prayer," by the Rev. Dr. G. VANCE SMITH.
TUESDAY, March 15.—"The Supreme Moral Law," by the Rev. W. BINNS.
FRIDAY, March 18.—"Man the Offspring of God," by the Rev. H. W. CROSSKEY, F.G.S.
TUESDAY, March 22.—"Salvation," by the Rev. ALEX. GORDON, M.A.
FRIDAY, March 25.—"Jesus Christ," by the Rev. C. BEARD, B.A.
TUESDAY, March 29.—"The Bible," by the Rev. Prof. J. ESTLIN CARPENTER, M.A.
FRIDAY, April 1.—"The Religious Life," by the Rev. T. W. FRECKLETON.
TUESDAY, April 5.—"The Church," by the Rev. H. IERSON, M.A.
FRIDAY, April 8.—"The Future Life," by the Rev. C. WICKSTEED, B.A.
Each Lecture will be preceded by a short Service, consisting of a hymn and prayer. To commence at four o'clock in the afternoon. Tickets admitting to the Course (free) may be obtained from Messrs. Smart and Allen, 9, London House-yard, Paternoster-row; Messrs. Clarke and Co., 13, Fleet-street; and at the Office of the Association, 37, Norfolk-street, Strand, London.

WESTBOURNE-PARK INSTITUTE, Porchester-road, Bayswater, W. (nearly opposite Royal Oak Station). President—JOHN CLIFFORD, M.A., LL.B., B.Sc.—Dr. B. W. RICHARDSON, F.R.S., will deliver a COURSE of THREE LECTURES on "Food and its Digestion," commencing on MONDAY EVENING, March 7, when the Hon. and Rev. W. H. FREMANTLE, M.A., of St. Mary's, Bryanston-square, will take the Chair at 8.15. The remaining lectures will be given on March 14—Chairman, Rev. Canon Farrar, D.D., and March 21—Chairman, Rev. Dr. Hermann Adler.—Admission to each Lecture, One Shilling; reserved seats, 2s.; for the Course, 2s. and 4s. 6d.

THE AFGHAN WAR.—FUND for the RELIEF of the WIDOWS and ORPHANS of all those who have fallen, or may yet fall, during the war, and on whose behalf the Committee earnestly APPEAL to their fellow-countrymen for HELP.

Applications have already been made for relief from 88 widows with 166 children, as against 90 widows with 142 sufferers from the late Zulu war, for whom over £29,000 was subscribed.

COMMITTEE.
H.R.H. The Duke of CAMBRIDGE, K.G

Lieut.-Gen. Sir John Adye.	Gen. Sir Archibald Little.
Gen. Mark Kerr Atherley.	Maj.-Gen. Sir Peter Lumsden.
Maj.-Gen. Sir Michael Biddulph	The Earl of Lytton.
Hon. Sir James Brind.	Gen. Lord Napier of Magdala.
Lieut.-Gen. Sir Samuel Browne.	Lieut.-Gen. Sir Henry Norman.
Viscount Cranbrook.	The Earl of Northbrook.
Colonel Sir Andrew Clarke.	Sir Lewis Pelly.
Maj.-Gen. Lord Chelmsford.	Lieut.-Gen. Sir Dighton Probyn.
Sir R. H. Davies.	Maj.-Gen. Sir Richard Pollock.
Sir Barrow Ellis.	Maj.-Gen. Sir Frederick Roberts.
The Marquess of Hartington.	Sir Nathaniel de Rothschild, Bt.
Sir Arthur Hobhouse.	Hon. Edward Stanhope, M.P.
Maj.-Gen. G. V. Johnson.	W. S. Seton-Karr, Esq.
Colonel Sir Charles Keyes.	Sir Alexander Taylor.
Lord Lawrence.	Thos. H. Thornton, Esq.
Lieut.-Gen. R. C. Lawrence.	

Captain James Gildea, 20, Stafford-terrace, Kensington, W., to whom all communications should be addressed.

TWENTY-SIXTH LIST OF SUBSCRIPTIONS.

	£ s. d.		£ s. d.
Amount already advertised	2,959 2 4		
Her Majesty the Queen		Collection at Charlynch, Bridgwater	3 10 0
Proceeds of the Assault at Arms given at the Royal Albert Hall, on 1st February, by the Staff of the Aldershot Gymnasium, per Major Cleather, Inspector of Gymnasia	511 10 0	Additional collection made by Mrs. S. Brown amongst her friends and fellow-servants	2 7 6
Miss Mary M'Muth	14 13 2	Captain H. Wylie	2 2 0
Officers Royal Artillery, Aldershot	10 0 0	John Davis, Esq.	2 2 0
Miss L. D. Lambton	8 0 0	John Denunce, Esq.	2 2 0
W. Jennings, Brauly, Esq.	5 0 0	Lieut.-General W. A. Crommelin, C.B.	1 1 0
J. Bassett, Esq.	5 0 0	Bushby Jamieson, Esq.	0 10 6
		Collection at Brockdish Church, Scole	0 7 0

CORRECTION.—For Col. Sir C. Keyes £30 9s., read Messrs. Fruhling and Goschen £20 5s., and Col. Sir C. Keys £4 4s.
March 4, 1881. JAMES GILDEA, Treasurer.

Subscriptions to the account of "The Afghan War Relief Fund" are received by the Bank of England, the Alliance Bank, Messrs. Barclay, Bevan, and Co.; Messrs. John Brown and Co.; the Capital [...]

LEGAL and GENERAL LIFE ASSURANCE OFFICE.
NOTICE IS HEREBY GIVEN, that the ANNUAL GENERAL MEETING of this Society will be held at this Office, on TUESDAY, the 22nd day of March instant, at 2 o'clock precisely. At such Meeting three vacancies, then to be created by the retirement in rotation of Joseph Henry Dart, Esq., James Parker Deane, Esq., Q.C., D.C.L., and Frederick John Blake, Esq., will be filled up. Two vacancies in the office of Auditor, caused by the retirement in rotation of Arthur Kekewich, Esq., Q.C., and Edward Amor Bush, Esq., will also be filled up at such meeting.

Saturday, 5th. March, 1881

Down early this morning after a restless night, Holmes as usual
monopolizing The Times. I rarely get a chance to look at it
until after he has cut it up for his own reference files. The
other papers had long accounts in their "Crime Reports" and the
Daily Telegraph, Standard and Daily News all had leading articles
on the "Brixton Mystery." To spite Holmes, and because there
was some information in them which was new to me, I cut out the
articles for my own scrapbook. Holmes then told me that he had
seen them already and was amused by the inevitable credit given
to Lestrade & Gregson. If the man was caught, it would be *On est trouve
toujours un plus*
on account of their exertions; if he escaped, it would be in *sot que l'admire*
spite of them, he said - heads I win and tails you lose!

    We were interrupted, much to the disgust of our landlady *The Baker Street
Division of
the
(and myself), by the appearance of half a dozen of the dirtiest *detective
and most ragged street Arabs that I have ever clapped eyes on. *police force.*
Having called them to order, Holmes questioned one, called *The rest are
Wiggins, and learnt that they had not yet found whatever it *in future
to wait
was Holmes wanted. He gave each a shilling and told them to go *in the
street*
on trying and to come back with a better report next time.
He remarked to me that there was more work to be got out of one
of those little beggars than out of a dozen of the police
force, for whereas the mere sight of an official-looking
person sealed men's lips, these youngsters could go everywhere
and hear everything. *They are as sharp as needles
All they want is organisation*

Just as they left, Gregson arrived, burst into our
sitting-room, seized Holmes's unresponsive hand and proudly
told us that the fellow we wanted was under lock and key.
Holmes looked anxious and asked the man's name. It was Arthur
Charpentier, sub-lieutenant in Her Majesty's Navy, announced
Gregson. Sighing with relief, Holmes offered Gregson a cigar
and some whisky with water and asked him how he managed it.

The detective was very complacent, talked about the mental
strain of the case, which Holmes, as a fellow brain-worker,
would understand, and chuckled so heartily over the thought of
Lestrade going off on the wrong track after Stangerson, that
he choked on his cigar. When he had recovered, he boasted that
it was not Tobias Gregson's way to sit idly waiting for
information to be volunteered. Did we remember the hat beside
the dead man, he asked, and was crestfallen when Holmes quoted
the manufacturer's name and address: John Underwood and Sons,
129, Camberwell Road. He asked if Holmes had been there, and
when Holmes said, no, pompously advised my companion never to
neglect a chance.

Smart - very smart

Gregson had discovered from Underwood the address to which
the hat had been sent: E.J. Drebber, Charpentier's Boarding
Establishment, Torquay Terrace. He had interviewed Madame
Charpentier, got the full story from her and arrested her son.
He had taken shorthand notes of her statement and showed us a
copy of the transcript for his official report. Holmes was
quick to congratulate him with great warmth.

*We will make something
of Gregson yet*

Metropolitan Police.

4th March. 18 81

Death of Enoch. J. Drebber at 3. Lauriston Gardens, Brixton
Interview with Madame Charpentier

Called upon Madame Charpentier, at Charpentier's Boarding Establishment, Torquay Terrace. Found her pale and distressed. Her daughter was in the room - uncommonly fine girl, looking rather red about the eyes.

Gregson: Have you heard of the mysterious death of your late boarder, Mr. Enoch J. Drebber, of Cleveland?

Mdme Charpentier nodded. Daughter burst into tears.

Gregson: At what o'clock did Mr. Drebber leave your house for the train?

Mdme Charpentier: (agitated) At eight o'clock. His secretary, Mr. Stangerson, said that there were two trains - one at 9.15 and one at 11.00. He was to catch the first.

Gregson: And was that the last which you saw of him?

Mdme Charpentier: (changing colour and hesitating) Yes.

Daughter: (calmly, after a pause) No good can ever come of falsehood mother. Let us be frank with the gentleman. We did see Mr. Drebber again.

Mdme Charpentier: (greatly disturbed) God forgive you! You have murdered your brother.

Daughter: (firmly) Arthur would rather we spoke the truth.

Gregson: You had best tell me all about it now. Half-confidences are worse that none. Besides, you do not know how much we know of it.

Mdme Charpentier: On your head be it, Alice! I will tell you all,

John Underwood & Sons,
129, Camberwell Road,
Camberwell, London.

Hat-makers

To : Enoch J Drebber
Charpentier's Boarding Establishment
Torquay Terrace.
Camberwell.

1 Gentleman's top hat, as ordered,
and paid

John Underwood.

J. Underwood & Sons
Hatmakers.

129 CAMBERWELL ROAD

sir. Do not imagine that my agitation on behalf of my son arises from any fear lest he should have had a hand in this terrible affair. He is utterly innocent of it. My dread is, however, that in your eyes and in the eyes of others he may appear to be compromised. That, however, is surely impossible. His high character, his profession, his antecedents would all forbid it.

Gregson: Your best way is to make a clean breast of the facts. Depend upon it, if your son is innocent he will be none the worse.

Mdme Charpentier: Perhaps, Alice, you had better leave us together. (The daughter withdrew.) Now, sir, I had no intention of telling you all this, but since my poor daughter has disclosed it I have no alternative. Having once decided to speak, I will tell you all without omitting any particular.

Gregson: It is your wisest course.

Mdme Charpentier: Mr. Drebber has been with us nearly three weeks. He and his secretary, Mr. Stangerson, had been travelling on the Continent. I noticed a Copenhagen label upon each of their trunks, showing that had been their last stopping place. Stangerson was a quiet, reserved man, but his employer, I am sorry to say, was far otherwise. He was coarse in his habits and brutish in his ways. The very night of his arrival he became very much the worse for drink, and, indeed, after twelve o'clock in the day he could hardly ever be said to be sober. His manners towards the maid-servants were disgustingly free and familiar. Worst of all, he speedily assumed the same attitude towards my daughter, Alice, and spoke to her more than once in a way which, fortunately, she is too innocent to understand. On one occasion he actually seized her in his arms and embraced her - an outrage which caused his own secretary to reproach him for his unmanly conduct.

Gregson: Why did you stand all this? I suppose that you can get rid of your boarders when you wish.

Mdme Charpentier: (blushing) Would to God that I had given him notice on the very day that he came. But it was a sore temptation. They were paying a pound a day each - fourteen pounds a week, and this is the slack season. I am a widow, and my boy in the navy has cost me much. I grudged to lose the money. I acted for the best. This last was too much, however, and I gave notice to leave on account of it. That was the reason of his going.

Gregson: Well?

Mdme Charpentier: My heart grew light when I saw him drive away. My son is on leave just now, but I did not tell him anything of all this, for his temper is violent, and he is passionately fond of his sister. When I closed the door behind them a load seemed to be lifted from my mind. Alas, in less than an hour there was a ring at the bell, and I learned that Drebber had returned. He was much excited, and evidently the worse for drink. He forced his way into the room, where I was sitting with my daughter, and then made some incoherent remark about having missed the train. He then turned to Alice, and before my very face proposed to her that she should fly with him. "You are of age," he said, "and there is no law to stop you. I have money enough and to spare. Never mind the old girl here, but come along with me now straight away. You shall live like a princess." Poor Alice was so frightened that she shrank away from him, but he caught her by the wrist and endeavoured to draw her towards the door. I screamed, and at that moment my son Arthur came into the room. What happened then I do not know. I heard oaths and the confused sounds of a scuffle. I was too terrified to raise my head. When I did look up I saw Arthur standing in the doorway laughing, with a stick

in his hand. "I don't think that fine fellow will trouble us again,"

he said. "I will just go after him and see what he does with himself."

With those words he took his hat and started off down the street. The

next morning we heard of Mr. Drebber's mysterious death.

Gregson: At what hour did your son return?

Mdme Charpentier: I do not know.

Gregson: Not know?

Mdme Charpentier: No, he has a latch-key and he let himself in.

Gregson: After you went to bed?

Mdme Charpentier: Yes.

Gregson: When did you go to bed?

Mdme Charpentier: About eleven.

Gregson: So your son was gone at least two hours?

Mdme Charpentier: Yes.

Gregson: Possibly four or five?

Mdme Charpentier: Yes.

Gregson: What was he doing during that time?

Mdme Charpentier: (turning white) I do not know.

Quite exciting I suppose

No doubt he saw that the whole case hung upon the one point and he fixed her with his eye in that way he has always found effective with women.

Tobias Gregson.

Scotland Yard
5th March 1881

Suitcases belonging to Drebber
and Stangerson

Metropolitan Police.

6th March. 1881

Death of Enoch J. Drebber at 3 Lauriston Gardens, Brixton Arrest of Lieutenant Charpentier.

Lieutenant Charpentier was arrested this evening by Detective Gregson, accompanied by two officers. He was evidently dangerous and still carried the stout oak cudgel which the mother described him as having with him when he followed Drebber. When touched on the shoulder and warned to come quietly, Lieutenant Charpentier said boldly, "I suppose you are arresting me for being concerned in the death of that scoundrel Drebber." Nothing had been said to him of this matter, so that his alluding to it had a most suspicious aspect. The young man then volunteered a brief statement:

Statement by Sub-lieutenant Charpentier

Enoch Drebber was an unwelcome lodger in my mother's house for some weeks. He was a drunkard and a braggart, and had been bothering my sister Alice. On Thursday night ~~morning~~, I returned to the house to find the dastardly fellow assaulting my sister and attempting to force her against her will to submit to his beastly proposals. I rescued Alice from his foul clutches, hauled him into the road, gave him the shaking he deserved and told the coward what I would do to him if he ever came near the house again. To make sure the bla'guard cleared off, I

followed him for some while down the streets, until he perceived
me and took a cab in order to escape his just punishment. That was
the last I saw of him. On my way home, I met an old shipmate and
took a long walk with him. I did not get home till late.

When asked where this shipmate lived, Lieutenant Charpentier replied,
"Somewhere in Greenwich, that's all I know."

Summary of case

It is obvious that Lieutenant Charpentier followed Drebber as far
as the Brixton Road. There, a fresh altercation arose between them,
in the course of which Drebber must have received a blow from the
stick, in the pit of the stomach, which killed him without leaving
any mark. The night was so wet that no one was about. Charpentier
dragged the body of his victim into the empty house. As to the
candle and the blood, and the writing on the wall, and the ring,
these were clearly intended as so many tricks to throw the police
on to the wrong scent.

Tobias Gregson.

Saturday, 5th. March, continued

Just as we had concluded Gregson's account of his interview with Madame Charpentier and the arrest of Lieutenant Charpentier, who should appear but Lestrade, looking tired, untidy and far from his usual jaunty self. He had evidently come with the intention of seeing Holmes privately, for on observing Gregson he appeared embarrassed and fumbled nervously with his hat, muttering that this was a most extraordinary case. *An incomprehensible affair I think he called it.*

Gregson did not help. He enquired smugly whether Lestrade had yet managed to find the secretary Stangerson. Lestrade's answer was so unexpected that we were all three dumbfounded for a moment. He had found Joseph Stangerson, he said, murdered at Halliday's Private Hotel about six o'clock this morning.

Gregson sprang out of his chair and upset the remainder of his whisky and water. I stared in silence at Holmes, whose lips were compressed and his brows drawn over his eyes. The plot thickens, he muttered. Lestrade grumbled that it was thick enough already, and when Gregson queried the news, he replied petulantly that he had just come from the room and had been the first to discover what had occurred.

Holmes asked him to tell us what happened, which he did, and I later requested to see a copy of his report, since I was too flabbergasted to make my usual notes of everything he said at the time.

Metropolitan Police.

Death of Joseph Stangerson at Halliday's Hotel, Little George Street.
Report of Investigating Officer.

Further to the discovery in No. 3, Lauriston Gardens, Brixton, of

the body of Enoch J. Drebber, and being of the opinion that his

secretary, Joseph Stangerson, was concerned in the death of Drebber,

I set myself to find out what had become of Stangerson.

They had been seen together at Euston Station about half past

eight on the evening of the third. At two in the morning Drebber

had been found in the Brixton Road. The question which confronted

me was to find out how Stangerson had been employed between 8.30 and

the time of the crime, and what had become of him afterwards. I

telegraphed to Liverpool, giving a description of the man, and warning

them to keep a watch upon the American boats. I then set to work

calling upon all the hotels and lodging-houses in the vicinity of

Euston. It was obvious that if Drebber and his companion had become

separated, the natural course for the latter would be to put up somewhere

in the vicinity for the night, and then to hang about the station again

next morning.

I spent the whole of the evening of the fourth in making enquiries

entirely without avail. This morning I began very early, and at eight

o'clock I reached Halliday's Private Hotel, in Little George Street.

On my enquiry as to whether Mr. Stangerson was living there, I was at

[handwritten annotation in right margin:] Good to know that Gregson had passed on Madame Charpentier's description of the two men to his colleague

[handwritten annotation in right margin:] They would be likely to agree on some meeting place beforehand.

once answered in the affirmative. The management assumed that I was
the gentleman for whom Stangerson had apparently been waiting for
two days. I was informed that he was upstairs in bed and had asked
to be called at nine.

I said I would go up at once for it seemed to me that my sudden
appearance might shake his nerves and lead him to say something
unguarded. The Boots volunteered to show me the room. It was on the
second floor, and there was a small corridor leading up to it. The
Boots pointed out the door to me, and was about to go downstairs
again when I saw something that alerted me instantly. From under the
door there curled a little red ribbon of blood, which had meandered
across the passage and formed a little pool along the skirting at
the other side. I gave a cry, which brought the Boots back. He nearly
fainted when he saw it. The door was locked on the inside, but we
put our shoulders to it, and knocked it in.

The window of the room was open, and beside the window, all
huddled up, lay the body of a man in his nightdress. He was quite
dead, and had been for some time, for his limbs were rigid and cold.
When we turned him over, the Boots recognized him at once as being
the same gentleman who had engaged the room under the name of Joseph
Stangerson. The cause of death was a deep stab in the left side,
which must have penetrated the heart. Above the murdered man, on the
wall, written in letters of blood, was the word "RACHE.

The suspect intruder was seen by a milk boy, passing on his way
to the dairy, who happened to walk down the lane which leads from
the mews at the back of the hotel. He noticed that a ladder, which
usually lay there, was raised against one of the windows of the

I remember poor old Lestra_ saying that i_ made him fe_ sickish in spite of his 20 years experience

I could have told him that as soon as he mentioned the body

second floor, which was wide open. After passing, he looked back and

saw a man descend the ladder. He came down so quietly and openly that

the boy imagined him to be some carpenter or joiner at work in the

hotel. He took no particular notice of him, beyond thinking in his

own mind that it was early for him to be at work. He has an impression

that the man was tall, had a reddish face, and was dressed in a long,

brownish coat. He must have stayed in the room for some little time

after the murder, for we found blood-stained water in the basin,

where he had washed his hands, and marks on the sheets where he had

deliberately wiped his knife.

Tallies rather well with my original description wouldn't you say

There was nothing in the room which could furnish a clue to

the murderer, nor any apparent motif. Stangerson had Drebber's purse

in his pocket, but it seems that this was usual, as he did all the

paying. There was eighty-odd pounds in it, but nothing had been taken.

A list of Stangerson's effects and the contents of the room is attached.

G. Lestrade

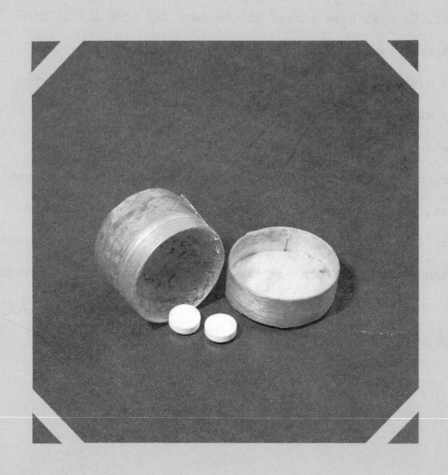

No. 6.

Special Report.

Reference to Papers.

Report of Investigating
Officer
G. Lestrade.

Metropolitan Police.

Scotland Yard STATION.   A   DIVISION

5th March 18 81

Effects of Joseph Stangerson, found on and about his
body, at Hallidays Hotel, Little George Street.

Purse, belonging to E. J. Drebber
Cash, contained in purse. £80. 2s 6d.
Telegram: dated 2nd February, from Cleveland
Novel: A. Rogue's Life, by Wilkie Collins, 1st ed. 1879
Gentleman's Pipe.
Small chip ointment box, containing two pills.

Andrew Couchman, (Sgt. 1-) Division).

G. Lestrade

POST OFFICE TELEGRAPHS.
(Inland Telegrams.)

A.

Prefix............ Code............

Obviously sent this telegram... must have received the description of Stangerson on or soon after his receipt of Gregson's ... from Gregson ... this interview with ... William Carpenter

Office of Origin and Service Instructions.

Immediate.

Brixton

Words		
39		

Sent At...Liverpool...

To....

By....

Charge 1/6

FROM

Lestrade
Scotland Yard, London

Please Write Distinctly.   Addresses Free.

Police Headquarters
Liverpool

PLEASE	WATCH	AMERICAN	BOATS	ESPECIALLY
GVION	LINE	FOR	PASSENGER	JOSEPH
STANGERSON	REQUIRED	URGENTLY	FOR	QUESTIONING
HEIGHT	SIX	FEET	SLIM	BUILD
SANDY	BROWN	HAIR	NEATLY	DRESSED
DARK	SUIT	AMERICAN	ACCENT	

BALANCE OF PORTERAGE REFUNDED

1/-
1/3
1/6

NOTICE TO THE SENDER OF THIS TELEGRAM.

This Telegram will be accepted for transmission subject to the Regulations made pursuant to the 15th Section of the Telegraph Act, 1868, and to the Notice printed at the back hereof.

(HARRISON & SONS, PRINTERS, LONDON.)

NOTICE TO THE SENDER OF THIS TELEGRAM.

1. The charge for transmission will cover the cost of delivery :—

   (a) If the address is within one mile from the Terminal Telegraph Office or within the limits of the Town Postal delivery of that Office when it is a Head Post Office.

   (b) If the Sender desires it to be forwarded by Post from the Terminal Telegraph Office and shall write the words " By Post " at the end of the address of the person to whom it is to be delivered.

2. The following charges will be made for the delivery of this Telegram in case the address be not within the above described limits and the Sender does not write the words, " By Post," at the end of such address :—

   (a) For delivery by Special Foot Messenger, at a distance less than three miles from the Terminal Telegraph Office, 6d. for each mile or part of a mile, reckoned from the boundary of the district of free delivery to the address of delivery.

   (b) For delivery by mounted Messenger, at a distance more than three miles from the Terminal Telegraph Office, 1s. for each mile or part of a mile, reckoned from the Terminal Telegraph Office to the address of delivery (except in some parts of Ireland, where the charge is at the rate of 8d. per mile).

3. If the Sender desires this Telegram to be forwarded by Train from the Terminal Telegraph Office, he must write the words " By Train " at the end of the address, and must pay the actual cost of the conveyance, if such cost be known, or must deposit 1s.

4. The Sender may prepay a reply not exceeding in length 40 words. In such case a Form of Pass will be handed to the Addressee. The Pass will, within two months from its date, frank any Telegram not exceeding in length the number of words stated on such Pass. If the Pass be not used the sum will be paid to any person forwarding such Pass, within two months from its date, to the Secretary, General Post Office, London.

5. A Telegram can be repeated if the Sender desires to adopt this security against the risk of error. The charge for repetition is one-half the charge for transmission, any fraction of 3d. being reckoned as 2d. If containing mercantile quotations or code words a telegram ought always to be repeated.

6. The Postmaster General will not be liable for any loss or damage which may be incurred or sustained by reason or on account of any mistake or default in the transmission or delivery of a Telegram.

7. All applications respecting this Telegram should be made within three months from the date of its transmission, after which period it will not be kept.

Hallidays Hotel
5th March 1881
Joseph Stangerson

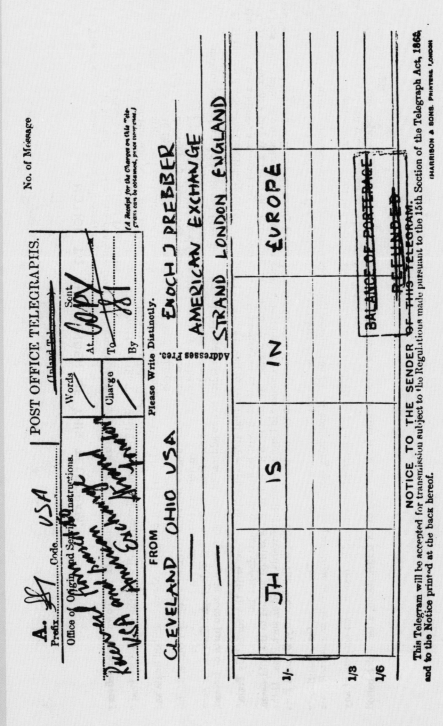

POST OFFICE TELEGRAPHS.

(Inland Telegrams.)

No. of Message

A. _VSA_

Prefx. Code.

Office of Origin and Service Instructions.

Words	Sent
	At. COPY
Charge	To. 181
	By.

(A Receipt for the Charge on this Telegram can be obtained, price twopence.)

Please Write Distinctly.

Addresses Free.

FROM

CLEVELAND OHIO VSA

ENOCH J PREBBER

AMERICAN EXCHANGE

STRAND LONDON ENGLAND

JH	IS	IN	EUROPE

1/-

1/3

1/6

BALANCE OF POSTPONE-

REFUNDED

NOTICE TO THE SENDER OF THIS TELEGRAM.

This Telegram will be accepted for transmission subject to the Regulations made pursuant to the 15th Section of the Telegraph Act, 1868, and to the Notice printed at the back hereof.

(HARRISON & SONS. PRINTERS, LONDON)

NOTICE TO THE SENDER OF THIS TELEGRAM.

1. The charge for transmission will cover the cost of delivery:—

    (a) If the address is within one mile from the Terminal Telegraph Office or within the limits of the Town Postal delivery of that Office when it is a Head Post Office.

    (b) If the Sender desires it to be forwarded by Post from the Terminal Telegraph Office and shall write the words " By Post " at the end of the address of the person to whom it is to be delivered.

2. The following charges will be made for the delivery of this Telegram in case the address be not within the above described limits and the Sender does not write the words " By Post " at the end of such address :—

    (a) For delivery by Special Foot Messenger, at a distance less than three miles from the Terminal Telegraph Office, 6d. for each mile or part of a mile, reckoned from the boundary of the district of free delivery to the address of delivery.

    (b) For delivery by mounted Messenger, at a distance more than three miles from the Terminal Telegraph Office, 1s. for each mile or part of a mile, reckoned from the Terminal Telegraph Office to the address of delivery (except in some parts of Ireland, where the charge is at the rate of 8d. per mile).

3. If the Sender desires this Telegram to be forwarded by Train from the Terminal Telegraph Office, he must write the words " By Train " at the end of the address, and must pay the actual cost of the conveyance, if such cost be known, or must deposit 1s.

4. The Sender may prepay a reply not exceeding in length 40 words. In such case a Form of Pass will be handed to the Addressee. The Pass will, within two months from its date, frank any Telegram not exceeding in length the number of words stated on such Pass. If the Pass be not used the sum will be paid to any person forwarding such Pass, within two months from its date, to the Secretary, General Post Office, London.

5. A Telegram can be repeated if the Sender desires to adopt this security against the risk of error. The charge for repetition is one-half the charge for transmission, any fraction of 3d. being reckoned as 2d. If containing mercantile quotations or code words a telegram ought always to be repeated.

6. The Postmaster-General will not be liable for any loss or damage which may be incurred or sustained by reason or on account of any mistake or default in the transmission or delivery of a Telegram.

7. All applications respecting this Telegram should be made within three months from the date of its transmission, after which period it will not be kept.

As soon as Lestrade had concluded his list of items found in
Stangerson's hotel room, Holmes sprang up from his chair with
an exclamation of delight, declaring, to the astonishment of
both detectives, that the small chip ointment box containing
the two pills completed his case. He was as certain of all the *of course*
There were
main facts, he said, from the time that Drebber parted from *details to be*
filled in
Stangerson at the station, up to the latest discovery, as if
he had seen them with his own eyes.

Promising to prove this, Holmes asked for the pills, which
Lestrade happened to have together with the purse and the *He failed to*
attach any
telegram, for he was going to leave them at the Police Station. *importance*
to these
Holmes asked me if they were ordinary pills. They were certainly
not but we agreed that they might be soluble in water.

Holmes then asked me to fetch up the poor little terrier
that Mrs. Hudson had been looking after since finding it lying
in the street from being hit by a four-wheeled growler. It was
old already and on the point of death. I placed it on a cushion
on the rug. Holmes cut one pill in half, dissolved one half in
a teaspoonful of water, told Lestrade, who said he couldn't see
what this had to do with the death of Stangerson, to be patient,
added a little milk to the water and offered it to the dog on
a saucer. The dog speedily licked the saucer dry. We all waited
for some startling effect but nothing happened, to Holmes's
increasing chagrin and the detectives' mutual delight.

It was incomprehensible that the very
pills I had suspected in the case of Drebber
should actually be found after the
death of Stangerson and yet
prove inert

Suddenly Holmes gave a shout, rushed to the box, cut the other pill in half, dissolved it, added milk and presented it to the terrier. The unfortunate creature's tongue seemed hardly to have been moistened in it before it gave a convulsive shiver in every limb, and lay as rigid and lifeless as if it had been struck by lightning.

Holmes explained with relief that he ought to have known that one of the two pills was deadly poison, the other entirely harmless. He then launched into a lengthy monologue about our failure to seize on the single real clue that was presented to us at the very beginning of the case and how all the outré and sensational details that had made the case more confusing and mysterious to us had served to enlighten him and to strengthen his conclusions. The most commonplace crime, he said, is often the most mysterious because it presents no new or special features from which deductions may be drawn. I was no clearer!

It is a mistake to confuse strangeness with mystery

Gregson listened impatiently, acknowledged that Holmes was a smart fellow, admitted both he and Lestrade were wrong, since neither Stangerson nor Charpentier could have committed the second murder, and then asked Holmes outright to name the murderer, if he could. Lestrade concurred, and I added that any delay might give the assassin time to commit some fresh atrocity.

Holmes frowned, then told us there would be no more murders and that he did know the name of the assassin. He hoped to lay hands on him soon but it would be a delicate matter, for the man was shrewd, desperate and supported by someone equally clever.

The mere knowing of his name was a small thing compared with the power of laying our hands on him

Both men were more than a match for the official force and would
vanish instantly if they suspected they were being pursued.
Meanwhile Holmes took all responsibility and promised to let
the detectives know everything as soon as he could.

Gregson flushed up to the roots of his flaxen hair, while
Lestrade's beady eyes glistened with curiosity and resentment.
Neither had time to speak, however, before there was a tap at
the door and young Wiggins introduced his insignificant and
unsavoury person, to say to Holmes that he had the cab downstairs.
Before I could ask about this, Holmes was flourishing a pair of
steel handcuffs in front of Lestrade, showing him how the spring
worked and saying that the police should introduce his own *They fasten in an instant!*
pattern at Scotland Yard. Lestrade said huffily that the old
pattern was just as good if they could find the man to put
them on. Holmes smiled and told Wiggins to ask the cabman to
step upstairs to help him with his boxes.

I was surprised to hear Holmes talk as though he were going
on a journey. He pulled out a small portmanteau and began to
strap it busily, when the cabman entered the room. Without
looking up or turning his head, Holmes asked the man to help
him with the buckle. The fellow came forward with a somewhat
sullen, defiant air and put down his hands to assist. At that
instant there was a sharp click, the jangling of metal, and
Holmes sprang to his feet again. "Gentlemen," he cried, with
flashing eyes, "let me introduce you to Mr. Jefferson Hope, the
murderer of Enoch Drebber and of Joseph Stangerson."

The whole thing occurred in a moment - so quickly that I had no time to realize it. I have a vivid recollection of that instant, of Holmes's triumphant expression and the ring of his voice, of the cabman's dazed, savage face, as he glared at the glittering handcuffs, which had appeared as if by magic upon his wrists. Then with an inarticulate roar of fury, the prisoner wrenched himself free of Holmes's grasp, and hurled himself through the window. Woodwork and glass gave way before him; but before he got quite through, Gregson, Lestrade & Holmes sprang upon him like so many staghounds.

He was dragged back into the room, and then commenced a terrific conflict. So powerful and so fierce was he that the four of us were shaken off again and again. He appeared to have the convulsive strength of a man in an epileptic fit. His face and hands were terribly mangled by his passage through the glass, but loss of blood had no effect in diminishing his resistance. It was not until Lestrade succeeded in getting his hand inside his neckcloth and half-strangling him that we made him realize that his struggles were of no avail; and even then we felt no security until we had pinioned his feet as well as his hands. That done, we rose to our feet breathless and panting.

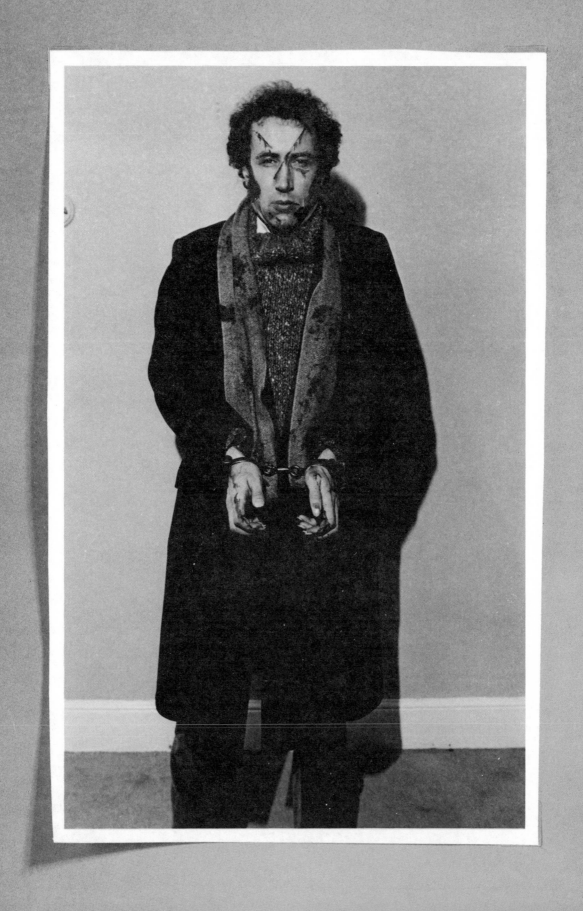

Scotland Yard
5th March 1881

Jefferson Hope
the evening of his capture
having shaved off his beard

The following pages have been typed up from a journal found
on Jefferson Hope when we seized him. The journal had
evidently been with him throughout most of his travels and
was falling apart; it was in a deplorable condition.
Many of the notes jotted down at the beginning were
almost illegible but towards the end there was this
coherent narrative, which he must have put together
when he reached London.

The narrative is a straightforward account of events.
I cannot help feeling that if these bare bones were
filled out with some descriptive colour and atmosphere,
there would be a story here as fine as and as dramatic
as anything I have ever read. It wants only the man
with the skill and the time to bring the tale alive.

Folded in the back of the journal was a
photograph and a slip of paper, poor mementoes to
which to cling!

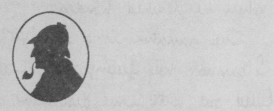

THE JOURNAL OF JEFFERSON HOPE

The first part of this story was told to me by John Ferrier,
when I met him in Salt Lake City in the summer of 1860. The
events that preceded our meeting seemed worth recording, for
they are the background to the tragic circumstances which have
so completely changed my destiny.

Ferrier journeyed west in the winter of 1846-47, with a band
of twenty-one companions, men, women and children, to seek new
farmlands. They travelled safely but not without incident until
they reached the barren and inhospitable alkali plain that
stretches from the Sierra Nevada to Nebraska and from the
Yellowstone River in the north to the Colorado upon the south.
     They had left one river and hoped to strike another but
either their map or their compass was wrong. Their water ran
out and one by one his companions died - Bender, Indian Pete,
Mrs. McGregor, Johnny Holmes, then little Lucy's mother and her
brother Bob. Lucy and Ferrier were the only survivors and she
being only five, with brown eyes, dainty shoes, a pink dress
and golden curls, he wrapped her in a bundle and carried her
over his shoulder. For three days and nights he tramped on
without rest and then collapsed in the shade of a rock on the
northern slope of the Sierra Blanco, from where they watched
the buzzards gather and prayed together and fell asleep.
     Ferrier woke to what he thought was delirium. Scouts from
a great caravan of settlers had sighted them and took them
down to their leader, a man of about thirty, with massive head
and resolute expression, called Brigham Young. His people,
explained Young, were the chosen of the Angel Merona, believers
in the sacred writings, drawn in Egyptian letters on plates of
beaten gold, which were handed unto the holy Joseph Smith at
Palmyra; they had come from Nauvoo, in the State of Illinois,
where they had been driven out of their temple. Ferrier had

heard the name of Nauvoo and knew them to be Mormons. He was
happy to agree to Young's terms, that they become believers in
the Mormons' own creed. It was the 4th. of May, 1847.

After many troubles, through which the people showed great
tenacity, they reached their destination, the promised land,
the broad valley of Utah. There, Young showed that he was an
able administrator and a resolute chief. Maps and buildings were
drawn up, the great temple rose swiftly and the land was
cultivated with crops of wheat. Ferrier had proved himself so
worthy on the journey that he was provided with as large and
fertile a piece of land as any of the settlers, with the
exception of Young himself and the four principal elders,
Stangerson, Kemball, Johnston and Drebber. He worked hard,
expanded his dwelling and increased the product of his farm.
In twelve years there were not half a dozen men in the whole
of Salt Lake City who could compare with him in wealth and no
name was better known. There was only one point on which he
offended the susceptibilities of his companions, in that he
would not set up a female establishment after their manner,
though he conformed to their religion in every other respect.

Meanwhile Lucy had adopted Ferrier's name and grew up
swiftly, helping him in everything and learning to manage a
mustang with all the ease and grace of a true child of the
West. She blossomed into as fair a specimen of American
girlhood as could be found in the whole Pacific coast.

She was eighteen when I met her, on the day she very nearly
came to grief beneath the hoofs and horns of a herd of fierce-
eyed, long-horned bullocks amidst whom she was accidently
trapped. I was riding past when I saw her startled horse
rearing and plunging. I could see that Lucy would soon lose
her hold and fall to her death, so I forced my way through the
drove, seized her horse's bridle, calmed the creature and
herself and led them out to safety.

I had seen the girl ride down from Ferrier's house and guessed who she was. I asked her to remember the Jefferson Hopes of St. Louis to her father, because if he was the same Ferrier, I knew that my father and he had once been pretty thick. She thanked me prettily for her rescue, invited me to visit their house whenever I liked, laughed at me when I was serious, gave me her hand and galloped away.

I had been among the Nevada Mountains prospecting for silver, and I and my companions were returning to Salt Lake City in the hope of raising capital enough to work some lodes which we had discovered. I had been as keen on the business as any of the others until I met this extraordinary girl and suddenly I was passionately in love with her. I visited the Ferriers often, told them tales of the outside world, of my pioneer days in California, strange tales of trapping, scouting, exploring for silver, ranching. Although Lucy often remained silent, I knew that she was falling as much in love with me as I with her.

There came a day that summer when I had to go back into the mountains with my companions. I determined to go for two months at the most and then return to claim Lucy for my wife. I won her father's consent to this, told Lucy of my plan, to which she agreed with joy, and said my farewells.

What happened during my absence, I heard later from John Ferrier himself, before his death. I knew that he would miss his daughter when I took her away but at the same time I knew also that he would never let her wed a Mormon, for he regarded their kind of marriage, with several wives, as a disgrace. But it was a dangerous thing to express an unorthodox opinion in the Land of the Saints in those days. The victims of persecution were themselves persecutors, more terrible than the Inquisition of Seville, invisible, omniscient, omnipotent; no man dared to whisper his doubts. The terror spread beyond Salt Lake City. As their supply of women ran out - for they needed a high female population to support their doctrine of polygamy - there were rumours of immigrant camps being attacked (not by Indians) and new women appeared in the harems of the Elders. Sinister bands of armed men, masked and cruel, roamed the mountains, seizing whomever they could find. The Danite Band, they were named, or sometimes the Avenging Angels. No one dared trust his neighbour, in case he was a member of this secret band.

One day, three weeks after I had left for the mountains, Brigham Young visited John Ferrier. He pointed out that the Mormons had befriended Ferrier and yet the stranger had ignored their principle of polygamy. Ferrier said that women had been few and that the company of his daughter had proved sufficient. Young talked of the reports he had heard that Lucy was to marry a Gentile, which the thirteenth rule in the code of Joseph Smith strictly forbade. He declared that it was to be a test of Ferrier's faith that he should marry his daughter to the young son either of Stangerson or Drebber. She must choose which. Ferrier asked for time to reach a decision and was given one month. As Young left the house, he turned to Ferrier and thundered: "It were better for you, John Ferrier, that you and she were now lying blanched skeletons upon the Sierra Blanco, than that you should put your weak wills against the orders of the Holy Four!"

Despite his fears for Lucy's safety, Ferrier swore that she should not be claimed by the Mormons. He would rather leave Utah, he said, than knuckle down to their Prophet. Meantime he sent a message by an aquaintance bound for the Nevada Mountains to warn me of the danger and to ask for my speedy return. That same day, he was visited by the two young men - Stangerson, with a long pale face, and four wives already; Drebber, bull-necked, with coarse and bloated features, and seven wives already. In front of Ferrier, they quarrelled as to who had prior claim on his daughter. Ferrier drove them out of the house in fury and they muttered curses as they went.

There had never been such a case of rank disobedience to the authority of the Elders. Ferrier's wealth and position would not protect him from their revenge. He tried to hide his fears from Lucy but the next morning, when he awoke, he discovered a small square of paper, pinned on the coverlet of his bed just over his chest, which was printed in bold, straggling letters: "Twenty-nine days are given you for amendment, and then - "

His heart was chilled, for his servants slept in an outhouse and the doors and windows had all been secured. The next day at breakfast, it was Lucy herself who noticed the number 28 scrawled with a burned stick in the centre of the ceiling. He sat up with his gun all the next night but on the following morning there was a great 27 painted on the outside of the door. In succeeding days, numbers appeared mysteriously on walls, on floors, sometimes on small placards stuck upon the garden gate or railing. One by one the numbers dwindled down, as Ferrier became more troubled and weary, until the morning on which the number 2 appeared on the wall of his house. He knew there was no escape, for he would quickly be hunted down if he tried to escape, with his limited knowledge of the mountains.

It was in the evening of that day that I returned, slithering on my belly between the guards that watched the house, and startled poor Ferrier almost out of his life. I knew it was a hornet's nest into which I'd put my head but those Mormons were not quite smart enough to catch a Washoe hunter! I had come as fast as possible on receiving Ferrier's note and I explained that we had to get out that very night and that I had a mule and two horses waiting nearby in the Eagle Ravine. We should push for Carson City, through the mountains, I said, and take all the money we could with us. Ferrier had to hand two thousand dollars in gold and five in notes. He carried the bag of money; Lucy brought a small bundle containing a few valued possessions; and I had the scant provisions and water.

    We left the house as silently as possible under cover
of dark and very nearly ran into some sentries whom we heard
talking: "Tomorrow at midnight," said one, "when the Whip-poor-
Will calls three times." "It is well," said the other, "shall
I tell Brother Drebber?" "Pass it on to him," said the first,
"and from him to the others. Nine to seven!" "Seven to five!"
repeated the other. They walked on and reached the animals.
Lucy rode the mule, Ferrier rode one horse and I led the other
along the precipitous route, with a great crag on one side and
a chaos of boulders on the other. We met with one more sentry
but got past him by saying that we were travellers for Nevada
by permission of the Holy Four and by answering his challenge
of "Nine to seven!" with the password "Seven to five!"

    Our dangers were not past, even when morning broke, for
we were still threatened by falling boulders and I knew that
the Avenging Angels would be upon our trail. All depended on
our speed in reaching Carson City but by the middle of the
second day our provisions had run out. I lit a fire, for we
were five thousand feet up and it was cold, and left Lucy and
Ferrier, while I went in search of game. It was two or three
hours before I shot a big-horn, and then I cut off one haunch
and part of the flank, lifted this on to my shoulder and started
back. But I had gone farther than I thought and became lost.
It was not until dark, and five hours after I had first left,
that I found myself near our camp. I called but there was no
reply. I found the remains of the fire but Lucy, Ferrier and
the animals were all gone.

    When I rekindled the fire, I saw by its light a mass of
hoof and footprints and a trail that led back towards Salt Lake
City. Then I saw the signs of a freshly dug grave. There was a
stick planted on it, with a sheet of paper stuck in the cleft
of it. The inscription confirmed that John Ferrier was dead.
I took the paper and have kept it ever since as a memento. The
good old man had been murdered and Lucy seized.

I resolved that my life should be devoted to retribution. It took me six days to toil back on foot to Eagle Canyon, from which I could see flags and signs of festivity in the streets of Salt Lake City. By chance, I encountered a Mormon called Cowper, to whom I had rendered a number of services. The fellow barely recognized my haggard features and then warned me that there was a warrant out against me from the Holy Four for assisting the Ferriers to escape. He told me also that Lucy Ferrier was married the day before to young Drebber, which explained the flags on the Endowment House. Drebber had won her against Stangerson's claims, though both men had apparently been in the party that shot Ferrier. Cowper added that Lucy was already more like a ghost than a woman and was not likely to survive for long, but what would her husband care about that, for he had married her chiefly for her father's money.

I stayed close to the city, in hiding, and within a month I heard of Lucy's death. The night before the burial, as Drebber's other wives sat up with the corpse, I crept into the city, entered the building secretly, brushed aside the women, kissed Lucy's cold forehead and snatched the ring from her finger, swearing that she should not be buried in that. I was gone again before they could raise the alarm.

Those events were more than twenty years ago - twenty years of pursuit and the hope of revenge. I hid in the mountains for some time, making sorties to put fear into the hearts of Drebber & Stangerson. A bullet through a window here, a boulder crashing down there. They sent expeditions to rout me out but I avoided them, and continued my harassment. In time, they feared to walk alone at night. But I could not survive indefinitely in this manner. I decided to recoup my strength and my resources in the old Nevada mines so that in a year's time I could pursue my revenge without privation but circumstances prevented me leaving the mines for nearly five years.

My desire for revenge did not abate in that time. I returned to Salt Lake City in disguise and there learnt that a schism in the Church had driven out several of the younger men including Drebber & Stangerson. Drebber had managed to depart with considerable wealth but Stangerson had left comparatively poor. No one knew their whereabouts.

I travelled endlessly throughout the United States in search of them, and my black hair turned grizzled, until one day, by chance, I glimpsed Drebber's face through a window in Cleveland, Ohio. Drebber saw and recognized me also and knew what I was after. He hurried before a justice of the peace, accompanied by Stangerson, who had become his private secretary, and represented to him that they were in danger of their lives from the jealousy and hatred of an old rival. That evening I was taken into custody, and not being able to find sureties, was detained for some weeks. When at last I was liberated, it was only to find that Drebber's house was deserted, and that he and his secretary had departed for Europe.

Once again I was foiled and it was some time before I was able to save enough money to continue the pursuit. At last I, too, departed for Europe, and tracked my enemies from city to city, working my way in any menial capacity, but never overtaking the fugitives. When I reached St. Petersburg, they had departed for Paris; and when I followed them there, I learned that they had just set off for Copenhagen. At the Danish capital I was again a few days late, for they had journeyed on to London, where at last I have succeeded in running them to earth.

They shall not escape.

John Ferrier
Salt Lake City
1859

Photograph found
with Journal of
Jefferson Hope
5th March 1881

JOHN FERRIER

FORMERLY OF SALT LAKE CITY

DIED AUGUST 4TH

1860

After we had recovered from the struggle and looked at Hope's notebook and mementoes, he was very affable, full of admiration for the way that Holmes had kept on his trail, said that Holmes should be made Chief of Police and asked him to unbind his legs, which he did. Gregson and Lestrade were disgusted.

We went by cab to the Police Station, where a white-faced, unemotional Inspector asked if Hope had anything he wished to say. Hope wanted to make a full statement immediately, in case he did not live until his trial. He was not thinking of suicide, he said, and asked me to put my hand against his chest. I could tell at once from the commotion that he had an aortic aneurism. Hope said it was the result of over-exposure and under-feeding among the Salt Lake Mountains and a doctor recently had said it would burst in a few days. Now that his work was done, he preferred to leave a truthful account and not to be remembered as a common cut-throat. I confirmed that he was near to death. He spoke very calmly and I can vouch for the accuracy of the account, for I have had access to Lestrade's notebook, in which the prisoner's words were taken down exactly as he uttered them.

There was only one secret he would not betray, when Holmes asked him; that was the name of his accomplice who came for the ring. When he had finished telling us everything else, the Inspector took him into custody and said that he would be brought before the Magistrates on Thursday next and we should attend.

<u>TRANSCRIPT OF HOPE'S STATEMENT</u>

It don't much matter to you why I hated these men; it's enough that they were guilty of the death of two human beings - a father and a daughter - and that they had, therefore, forfeited their own lives. After the lapse of time that has passed since their crime, it was impossible for me to secure a conviction against them in any court. I knew of their guilt though, and I determined that I should be judge, jury and executioner all rolled into one. You'd have done the same, if you have any manhood in you, if you had been in my place.

That girl was to have married me twenty years ago. She was forced into marrying Drebber, and broke her heart over it. I took the marriage ring from her dead finger, and I vowed that his last thoughts should be of the crime for which he was punished. I have carried it about with me, and have followed him and his accomplice over two continents until I caught them. They thought to tire me out, but they could not do it. If I die tomorrow, as is likely enough, I die knowing that my work in this world is done, and well done. They have perished, and by my hand. There is nothing left for me to hope for, or to desire.

They were rich and I was poor, so that it was no easy matter for me to follow them. When I got to London my pocket was about empty, and I found that I must turn my hand to something for my living. Driving and riding are as natural to me as walking, so I applied at a cab-owner's office, and soon got employment. I was to bring a certain sum a week to the owner, and whatever was over that I might keep for myself. There was seldom much over, but I managed to scrape along somehow. The hardest job was to learn my way about, for I reckon that of all the mazes that ever were contrived, this city is the most confusing. I had a map beside me though, and when once I had spotted the principal hotels and stations, I got on pretty well.

It was some time before I found out where my two gentlemen were living; but I inquired and inquired until at last I dropped across them. They were at a boarding house at Camberwell, on the other side of the river. When once I found them out, I knew that I had them at my mercy. I had grown my beard, and there was no chance of their recognizing me. I would dog them until I saw my opportunity. I was determined they should not escape me again.

They were very near doing it for all that. Go where they would about London, I was always at their heels. Sometimes I followed them on my cab, and sometimes on foot, but the former was the best, for then they could not get away from me. Only in the morning or late at night could I earn anything, so that I began to get behindhand with my employer. I did not mind that, however, as long as I could lay my hand upon the men I wanted.

They were very cunning, though. They must have thought that there was some chance of being followed, for they would never go out alone, and never after nightfall. During two weeks I drove behind them every day, and never once saw them separate. Drebber himself was drunk half the time but Stangerson was not to be caught napping. I watched them late and early but never saw the ghost of a chance; but I was not discouraged, for something told me that the hour had almost come. My only fear was that this thing in my chest might burst a little too soon and leave my work undone.

At last, one evening, I was driving up and down Torquay Terrace, as the street was called in which they boarded, when I saw a cab drive up to their door. Some luggage was brought out and Drebber & Stangerson followed it, and drove off. I whipped up my horse and kept within sight of them, feeling very ill at ease, for I feared that they were going to shift their quarters. At Euston Station they got out, and I left a boy to hold my horse and followed them on to the platform.* I heard them ask for the Liverpool train, and the guard answer that one had just gone, and there would not be another for some hours. Stangerson seemed to be put out at that, but Drebber was rather pleased than otherwise. I got so close to them in the bustle that I could hear every word that passed between them. Drebber said that he had a little business of his own to do, and that if the other would wait for him he would soon rejoin him.

*If no tickets were found upon either body
I suppose they never purchased any?

His companion remonstrated with him, and reminded him that they had resolved to stick together. Drebber answered that the matter was a delicate one, and that he must go alone. I could not catch what Stangerson said to that, but the other burst out swearing, and reminded him that he was nothing more than his paid servant, and that he must not presume to dictate to him. On that the secretary gave it up as a bad job and simply bargained with him that if he missed the last train he should rejoin him at Halliday's Private Hotel; to which Drebber answered that he would be back on the platform before eleven, and made his way out of the station.

The moment for which I had waited so long had at last come. I had my enemies within my power. Together they could protect each other, but singly they were at my mercy. I did not act, however, with undue precipitation. My plans were already formed. There is no satisfaction in vengeance unless the offender has time to realize who it is that strikes him, and why retribution has come upon him. I had my plans arranged by which I should make the man who had wronged me understand that his old sin had found him out. It chanced that some days before a gentleman who had been engaged in looking over some houses in the Brixton Road had dropped the key* of one of them in my carriage. It was claimed that same evening, and returned; but in the interval I had taken a moulding of it, and had a duplicate constructed, so that I had access to at least one spot in this great city where I could rely upon being free from interruption. How to get Drebber to that house was the problem I had now to solve.

He walked down the road and went into one or two liquor shops, staying for nearly half an hour in the last of them. When he came out, he staggered in his walk, and was evidently pretty well on. There was a hansom just in front of me, and he hailed it. I followed it so close that the nose of my horse was within a yard of his driver the whole way. We rattled across Waterloo Bridge and through miles of streets, until, to my astonishment, we found ourselves back in the terrace in which he had boarded. I could not imagine what his intention was in returning there; but I went on and pulled up my cab a hundred yards or so from the house. He entered it, and

* Whatever happened to the key?

& Madame Charpentier said they left her house at eight and were back within one hour, Lestrade said they were at Euston at 8.30. How does this half-hour fit in? Madame Charpentier must be mistaken as to one hour!

his hansom drove away. (At this point, Hope asked for a glass of water, for his mouth was dry with talking. He was handed one and he drank it down, saying afterwards that he felt better.)

Well, I waited for a quarter of an hour, or more, when suddenly there came a noise like people struggling inside the house. Next moment the door was flung open and two men appeared, one of whom was Drebber, and the other was a young man whom I had never seen before. This fellow had Drebber by the collar, and when they came to the head of the steps he gave him a shove and a kick which sent him half across the road. "You hound!" he cried, shaking his stick at him; "I'll teach you to insult an honest girl!" He was so hot that I think he would have thrashed Drebber with his cudgel, only that the cur staggered away down the road as fast as his legs would carry him. He ran as far as the corner, and then seeing my cab hailed me and jumped in.

"Drive me to Halliday's Private Hotel," said he.

When I had him fairly inside my cab, my heart jumped so with joy that I feared lest at this last moment my aneurism might go wrong. I drove along slowly, weighing in my own mind what it was best to do. I might take him right out into the country, and there in some deserted lane have my last interview with him. I had almost decided upon this, when he solved the problem for me. The craze for drink had seized him again, and he ordered me to pull up outside a gin palace. He went in, leaving word that I should wait for him. There he remained until closing time, and when he came out he was so far gone that I knew the game was in my own hands.

Don't imagine that I intended to kill him in cold blood. It would only have been rigid justice if I had done so, but I could not bring myself to do it. I had long determined that he should have a show for his life if he chose to take advantage of it. Among the many billets which I have filled in America during my wandering life, I was once janitor and sweeper-out of the laboratory at York College. One day the professor was lecturing on poisons, and he showed his students some alkaloid, as he called it, which he had extracted from some South American arrow poison, and which

was so powerful that the least grain meant instant death. I spotted
the bottle in which this preparation was kept, and when they were
all gone, I helped myself to a little of it. I was a fairly good
dispenser, so I worked this alkaloid into small, soluble pills, and
each pill I put in a box with a similar pill made without the poison.
I determined at the time that when I had my chance my gentlemen
should each have a draw out of one of these boxes, while I ate the
pill that remained. It would be quite as deadly and a good deal
less noisy than firing across a handkerchief. From that day I had
always my pill boxes about with me, and the time had now come when
I was to use them.

It was nearer one than twelve, and a wild, bleak night, blowing
hard and raining in torrents. Dismal as it was outside, I was glad
within - so glad that I could have shouted out from pure exultation.
If any of you gentlemen have ever pined for a thing, and longed for
it during twenty long years, and then suddenly found it within
your reach you would understand my feelings. I lit a cigar, and
puffed at it to steady my nerves, but my hands were trembling and
my temples throbbing with excitement. As I drove, I could see old
John Ferrier and sweet Lucy looking at me out of the darkness and
smiling at me, just as plain as I see you all in this room. All the
way they were ahead of me, one on each side of the horse, until I
pulled up at the house in the Brixton Road.

There was not a soul to be seen, nor a sound to be heard,
except the dripping of the rain. When I looked in at the window,
I found Drebber all huddled together in a drunken sleep. I shook
him by the arm, "It's time to get out," I said.

"All right, cabby," said he.

I suppose he thought we had come to the hotel that he had
mentioned, for he got out without another word, and followed me
down the garden. I had to walk beside him to keep him steady, for
he was still a little top-heavy. When we came to the door, I
opened it, and led him into the front room. I give my word that all
the way, the father and daughter were walking in front of us.

"It's infernally dark," said he, stamping about.

"We'll soon have a light," I said, striking a match and putting it to a wax candle which I had brought with me. "Now, Enoch Drebber," I continued, turning to him, and holding the light to my own face, "who am I?"

He gazed at me with bleared, drunken eyes for a moment, and then I saw horror spring up in them, and convulse his whole features, which showed me that he knew me. He staggered back with a livid face, and I saw the perspiration break out upon his brow, while his teeth chattered in his head. At the sight I leaned back against the door and laughed loud and long. I had always known that vengeance would be sweet, but I had never hoped for the contentment of soul which now possessed me.

"You dog!" I said; "I have hunted you from Salt Lake City to St. Petersburg, and you have always escaped me. Now at last your wanderings have come to an end, for either you or I shall never see tomorrow's sun rise." He shrunk still farther away as I spoke, and I could see on his face that he thought I was mad. So I was for the time. The pulses in my temples beat like sledge-hammers, and I believe I would have had a fit of some sort if the blood had not gushed from my nose and relieved me.

"What do you think of Lucy Ferrier now?" I cried, locking the door, and shaking the key in his face. "Punishment has been slow in coming, but it has overtaken you at last." I saw his coward lips tremble as I spoke. He would have begged for his life, but he knew well that it was useless.

"Would you murder me?" he stammered.

"There is no murder," I answered. "Who talks of murdering a mad dog? What mercy had you upon my poor darling, when you dragged her from her slaughtered father, and bore her away to your accursed and shameless harem."

"It was not I who killed her father," he cried.

"But it was you who broke her innocent heart," I shrieked, thrusting the box before him. "Let the high God judge between us. Choose and eat. There is death in one and life in the other. I shall take what you leave. Let us see if there is justice upon the earth, or if we are ruled by chance."

He cowered away with wild cries and prayers for mercy, but I drew my knife and held it to his throat until he had obeyed me. Then I swallowed the other, and we stood facing one another in silence for a minute or more, waiting to see which was to live and which was to die. Shall I ever forget the look which came over his face when the first warning pangs told him that the poison was in his system? I laughed as I saw it, and held Lucy's marriage ring in front of his eyes. It was but for a moment, for the action of the alkaloid is rapid. A spasm of pain contorted his features; he threw his hands out in front of him, staggered, and then, with a hoarse cry, fell heavily upon the floor. I turned him over with my foot, and placed my hand upon his heart. There was no movement. He was dead!

The blood had been streaming from my nose, but I had taken no notice of it. I don't know what it was that put it into my head to write upon the wall with it. Perhaps it was some mischievous idea of setting the police upon the wrong track, for I felt light-hearted and cheerful. I remembered a German being found in New York with "RACHE" written up above him, and it was argued at the time in the newspapers that the secret societies must have done it. I guessed that what puzzled the New Yorkers would puzzle the Londoners, so I dipped my finger in my own blood and printed it on a convenient place on the wall. Then I walked down to my cab and found that there was nobody about, and that the night was still very wild. I had driven some distance, when I put my hand into the pocket in which I usually kept Lucy's ring, and found that it was not there. I was thunderstruck at this, for it was the only memento that I had of her. Thinking that I might have dropped it when I stooped over Drebber's body, I drove back, and leaving my cab in a side street, I went boldly up to the house - for I was ready to dare anything rather than lose the ring. When I arrived there, I walked right into the arms of a police-officer who was coming out, and only managed to disarm his suspicions by pretending to be hopelessly drunk.

That was how Enoch Drebber came to his end. All I had to do then was to do as much for Stangerson, and so pay off John Ferrier's debt. I knew that he was staying at Halliday's Private Hotel, and I hung about all day, but he never came out. I fancy that he suspected something when Drebber failed to put in an appearance. He was cunning, was Stangerson, and always on his guard. If he thought he could keep me off by staying indoors he was very much mistaken. I soon found which was the window of his bedroom, and early next morning I took advantage of some ladders which were lying in the lane behind the hotel, and so made my way into his room in the grey of the dawn. I woke him up and told him that the hour had come when he was to answer for the life he had taken so long before. I described Drebber's death to him, and I gave him the same choice of the poisoned pills. Instead of grasping at the chance of safety which that offered him, he sprang from his bed and flew at my throat. In self-defence I stabbed him to the heart. It would have been the same in any case, for Providence would never have allowed his guilty hand to pick out anything but the poison.

I have little more to say and it's as well, for I am about done up. I went on cabbing it for a day or so, intending to keep at it until I could save enough to take me back to America. I was standing in the yard when a ragged youngster asked if there was a cabby there called Jefferson Hope, and said that his cab was wanted by a gentleman at 221B, Baker Street. I went round suspecting no harm, and the next thing I knew, this young man here had the bracelets on my wrists, and as neatly shackled as ever I saw in my life. That's the whole of my story, gentlemen. You may consider me to be a murderer; but I hold that I am just as much an officer of justice as you are.

(End of Statement)

* He must have known the danger from the experience of his accomplice whom I followed. Hope clearly had a death wish in coming to Baker Street

Slept very little last night. Holmes back late
and much melancholy scraping on his violin into
the early hours. Restless and up well before my usual
time. Morning papers full of the "Brixton Mystery"
but hardly time to finish breakfast before we were
invaded by scruffy urchins hired by Holmes to
ferret out unknown information. No sooner were
they gone than Gregson appeared, elated with the
news that he had arrested Lt. Charpentier for the
murder of Drebber, after taking a long statement
from Charpentier's mother, who owned the boarding
house where Drebber had stayed. Gregson had
scarcely finished crowing when Lestrade arrived
with news that he had found Stangerson dead in
Halliday's Private Hotel. This was splendid fun.
It knocked Gregson's theory, because his current
suspect in the case was in custody at the time
and it stumped Lestrade, who had supposed
Stangerson to have been Drebber's murderer. By
the time Holmes had finished off Mrs. Hudson's
poor old stray with some poisonous pills found

near Stangerson's body, the urchins brought in a cabby who was seized on by Holmes as the real culprit. We had quite a tussel with this fellow Hope before he was secured and then we got the full story out of him before we took him down to the police station. Mrs. Hudson did us rather proud this evening with a cold chicken and ham but spoilt the celebration by producing pineapple for dessert.

Sunday. 6th March.   1881

Up late this morning after the excitement of the
last two days. Holmes out and the coffee cold.
Mrs. Hudson is not to be trifled with on Sundays
and makes no concessions to a weary lodger! Feeling
that I wanted some congenial company, went to the
Northumberland Baths and gathered quite an interested
group about me with my vivid description of events.
All rather impressed with my inside knowledge. Quite
like old times!

Monday. 7th. March.

Gregson round this morning to confirm that Hope
had died in his cell the very night after his capture.
I was hardly surprised to hear that his aneurism
had burst. Gregson upset, because he has been
cheated of his star exhibit. Back to routine today
and Mrs. Hudson in a better humour. Two visitors
for Holmes but neither stayed long and he asked
Mrs. Hudson to take me up a fresh pot of coffee while
I was in my bedroom. Later. Holmes very relaxed.

Tuesday, 8th March.

Have definitely decided to gather together all the circumstances of the case, the papers and as much of the evidence as I can recover, in order to publish an account. I need a connection in the world of publishing. Perhaps Holmes has one.

What you do in this world is a matter of no consequence - The question is what you can make people believe you have done.

Discussed the case with Holmes and we tied up the loose ends.
Holmes believed that Gregson & Lestrade would be wild about
Hope's death, as it deprived them of their "grand advertisement."
I rather pleasantly replied that I did not see that they had
very much to do with his capture. Holmes shrugged this off
and said that he wouldn't have missed the best case he'd ever
known; simple as it was, he said, there were several most
instructive points about it. Back to his old arrogance!

He launched into an explanation as to how most people
only reason forward (arguing a result from a train of events)
and how very few are able to reason backward (arguing the
events from a particular result). Of course, I said that I
understood, hoping he would illustrate his point, which he
did, and I took down his explanation word for word:

I hardly expected that you would

Summary by Holmes: This was a case in which you were given the
result and had to find everything else for yourself. To begin
at the beginning, I approached the house on foot, and with my
mind entirely free from all impressions. I began by examining
the roadway, and there I saw the marks of a cab, which, I
ascertained by inquiry, must have been there during the night.
I walked slowly down the garden path, composed of a clay soil,
peculiarly suitable for taking impressions.* I saw the heavy
footmarks of the constable but also the track of the two men

Narrow gauge meant London growler - not gentleman's brougham

* *Trampled slush to you, but every mark had meaning. The art of tracing footsteps is sadly neglected, but with practice has become second nature to me.*

who had first passed through the garden. It was easy to tell they had been there before the others, because in places their marks had been obliterated by those upon the top of them. This told me that my nocturnal visitors were two in number, *Calculated from the length of his stride* one remarkable for his height and the other fashionably dressed, to judge from the small and elegant impression left by his boots.

On entering the house, this last inference was confirmed. My well-booted man lay before me. The tall one, then, had done the murder. *if murder there was* There was no wound upon the dead man's person, but *Victims of heart disease or other natural causes never appear agitated* the agitated expression upon his face assured me that he had foreseen his fate. Having sniffed the dead man's lips, I detected a slightly sour smell and I argued that the poison *Forcible administration of poison, not new in criminal annals. See Dolsky in Odessa, and Leturier in Montpellier* had been forced upon him from the hatred and fear expressed upon his face. By the method of exclusion, I had arrived at this result, for no other hypothesis would meet the facts.

Robbery had not been the object of the murder, for nothing was taken. Was it politics, then, or was it a woman? Political *The tracks all over the room showed he had been there all the time* assassins are only too glad to do their work and to fly. This murder had, on the contrary, been done most deliberately. It must have been a private wrong, which called for such a methodical revenge. The inscription on the wall was too evidently a blind. When the ring was found, it settled the question. Clearly the murderer had used it to remind his victim of some dead or absent woman.

I made a careful examination of the room, which confirmed me in my opinion as to the murderer's height, and furnished me

with the additional details as to the Trichinopoly cigar and
the length of his nails. I had already concluded, since there
were no signs of a struggle, that the blood which covered the
floor had burst from the murderer's nose in his excitement.
I saw that the track of blood coincided with the track of his
feet. It is seldom that any man, unless he is very full-blooded,
breaks out in this way through emotion, so I hazarded the *Events proved that I had judged*
opinion that the criminal was a robust and ruddy-faced man. *correctly*

Having left the house, I did what Gregson had neglected.
I telegraphed to the head of police at Cleveland, limiting my
inquiry to the circumstances connected with the marriage of
Enoch Drebber. The answer was conclusive. It told me that
Drebber had already applied for the protection of the law *I knew then that I held the clue*
against an old rival in love, named Jefferson Hope, and that *to the mystery in my hand.*
this same Hope was at present in Europe. *and all that remained was to secure the murderer*

I had already determined that the man who entered the house
with Drebber was none other than the man who had driven the cab.
The marks in the road showed me that the horse had wandered on
in a way which would have been impossible had there been anyone
in charge of it. Where could the driver be, unless he were
inside the house? It is absurd to suppose that any sane man
would carry out a deliberate crime under the eyes of a third
person, and suppose one man wished to dog another through London,
what better means could he adopt than to turn cab-driver. All
these considerations led me to the irresistible conclusion that
Jefferson Hope was to be found among the jarveys of the Metropolis.

If he had been one, there was no reason to believe he had ceased to be; nor was there any reason to suppose he was going under an assumed name: why should he change his name in a country where no one knew his original one? I therefore sent my Street Arab detective corps systematically to every cab proprietor in London until they ferreted out the man that I wanted. The murder of Stangerson was entirely unexpected but could hardly have been prevented. Through it, I came into possession of the pills, the existence of which I had already surmised. You see, the whole thing is a chain of logical sequences without break or flaw.

For once, I gave Holmes unstinted praise and told him that his merits should be publicly recognized and that I would publish an account of the case if he wouldn't do it himself. He said I could do what I liked and handed me that day's <u>Echo</u>, laughing at a paragraph which gave all the credit to Gregson & Lestrade, and reminding me of what he had told me when we started. I said that it didn't matter because I had all the facts in my journal and the public should know them. In the meantime, I said, he should be contented with the consciousness of success, like the Roman miser. I was rather pleased to be able to quote this bit of classical learning to my friend: "Everyone scorns me but I'm quite happy to stay at home and admire my moneybox!"

"Populus me sibilat, at mihi plaudo

"Ipse domi simul ac nummos contemplar in arca."

FORM FOR AMERICAN MESSAGES ONLY

No. of Message _5492_

Station _BRIXTON_

Prefix _SY/SH_ Code Time _1315_ WORDS TO BE SIGNALLED _91_

Received _BO_ m

Finished _BIS_ m

Date _4th MARCH_ 18 _81_

Sent to _CLEVELAND_ Station.

by me _Sy_ Clerk.

Message ....

Repeating ... _KEF GREGSON ACCOUNT OF SCOTLAND YARD_

Reply .... _"QUERIED BY SCOTLAND YARD"_

To be paid out _6_ ...

(DQ—MM)   (Address)   (MM—PQ)

Counter Clerk's Initials ......

Total .....

FROM

Name and Address of the Sender of the Message.
HOLMES 221B BAKER STREET LONDON W

TO

Name and Full Address of the Person to whom the Message is to be delivered.
POLICE HEADQUARTERS CLEVELAND OHIO USA

DQ

FURTHER TO SCOTLAND YARD TELEGRAM OF SAME DATE IN CASE OF ENOCH J DREBBER OF CLEVELAND OHIO FOUND DEAD IN LONDON HOUSE STOP SUSPECT THAT THERE IS A WOMAN INVOLVED IN THE CASE STOP PLEASE SUPPLY ANY INFORMATION WITH REGARD TO THE PROBABLE MARRIAGE OF DREBBER OR WITH REGARD TO ANY RECENT CIRCUMSTANCES INVOLVING DREBBER AND A WOMAN AND A THIRD PARTY STOP URGENTLY REQUIRE NAMES OF WOMAN AND THIRD PARTY STOP NAME OF JOSEPH STANGERSON ALREADY KNOWN AND NOT REQUIRED STOP PLEASE RETURN ANSWER TO BAKER STREET ADDRESS SOONEST STOP

THIS MESSAGE IS PAID FOR AS AN ORDINARY UNPACKED MESSAGE.

The latter part of this request only applies to messages requiring a deposit.

Please to Telegraph the above Message according to the conditions endorsed hereon ; and to transfer such Message, at London, to be forwarded, subject to the endorsed conditions, to the above Address ; for which latter purpose I have deposited _____

You are requested, before signing, to read the Conditions of the Contract on the back.

Sherlock Holmes

Baker Street

Signature and Address of Sender.

NOTICE TO THE PUBLIC.

CONDITIONS AS TO MESSAGES TO AMERICA.

The Companies to which the American Cables belong will not incur or accept any liability whatsoever, either for the due transmission of Telegrams to the Cables, or for their safe delivery at their destination; nor will they accept any liability arising from delay or stoppage by reason of any accident to the Cables or Instruments, or from errors caused by indistinct handwriting, nor will they consent to be liable, under any circumstances, for any sum whatever, as damages or otherwise, for loss resulting from errors, mistakes, delays, or other causes in respect to any Message entrusted to them, beyond the return of that portion of the charge accruing to them out of the amount received, and then only in case the Message should fail in transmission when in their hands.

FORM FOR AMERICAN MESSAGES ONLY

No. of Message 1776 Copy

MESSAGE RECEIVED FROM AMERICA

Station _____

Prefix _____	Code Time _____	WORDS TO BE SIGNALLED. } _____	Message .... „ „
	Date _____ 187		Repeating ... „ „
Received _____ m }	Sent to _____ Station.		Reply .... „ „
Finished _____ m }	by me _____ Clerk.		To be paid out _Received 5·30_
(DQ—MM) = (Address)	(MM—PQ)	Counter Clerk's Initials ...., }	Total ...... „ „

FROM

Name and Address of the Sender of the Message. { MESSAGE RECEIVED FROM CLEVELAND OHIO USA 4 MARCH 1841

TO

Name and Full Address of the Person to whom the Message is to be delivered. { SHERLOCK HOLMES 221B BAKER STREET LONDON ENGLAND

DQ

CONFIRM NO CRIMINAL RECORD ON DREBBER AS
TELEGRAPHED TO SCOTLAND YARD EARLIER STOP FURTHER
INQUIRY ON MARRIAGE OR WOMAN INDICATES THAT DREBBER APPLIED FOR
THE PROTECTION OF THE LAW AGAINST AN OLD RIVAL IN LOVE
NAMED JEFFERSON HOPE STOP HOPE WAS TAKEN INTO
TEMPORARY CUSTODY STOP

THIS MESSAGE IS PAID FOR AS AN ORDINARY UNPACKED MESSAGE.

The latter part of this request only applies to messages requiring a deposit. { *Please to Telegraph the above Message according to the conditions endorsed hereon ; and to transfer such Message, at London, to be forwarded, subject to the endorsed conditions, to the above Address ; for which latter purpose I have deposited _____*

You are requested, before signing, to **read the Conditions** { _____ } Signature and Address of Sender.
of the Contract on the back.

NOTICE TO THE PUBLIC.

CONDITIONS AS TO MESSAGES TO AMERICA.

The Companies to which the American Cables belong will not incur or accept any liability whatsoever, either for the due transmission of Telegrams to the Cables, or for their safe delivery at their destination; nor will they accept any liability arising from delay or stoppage by reason of any accident to the Cables or Instruments, or from errors caused by indistinct handwriting, nor will they consent to be liable, under any circumstances, for any sum whatever, as damages or otherwise, for loss resulting from errors, mistakes, delays, or other causes in respect to any Message entrusted to them, beyond the return of that portion of the charge accruing to them out of the amount received, and then only in case the Message should fail in transmission when in their hands.

SPECIAL PREPAID ADVERTISEMENTS.

20 WORDS 1s.; 3 INSERTIONS 2s. 6d.
and 4d. per Insertion for each additional Eight Words.

LOST, FOUND, MISSING, &c.

BUSINESSES TO BE DISPOSED OF.

FOR SALE.

AR.

ICE.

IANS.

ht days
l corre-
ews, in
f those
had an
the re-
which
It was
ng Pro-
ld be al-
tiations
w begin
omplete
rom the
and no
p there
emands
s little
nts are
le; and
of the
attack
ements
ndard's
tem-
eported
vilians,
to the
sort of
scaped
State,
Lam-
castle
a more
Dr.
named
ces of
ion of
unded.
ted by
arged
aggon
They
t. On
taken
s then
s away
ntered
death
rough
New-
ed he
ooded,
hours.
ments,
rivers
New-
Boers
unger
singly
on the
off to
Boer
t one
was
neral
f his
s.

rmis-
s be-
neral,
rpose
the
late

GENERAL NEWS.

The Thames River Bill.

It is expected that there will be an animated debate to-morrow in the House of Commons on the Thames River Bill. Should the second reading be agreed to it will be proposed to refer the measure to a Select Committee.

Sir Garnet Wolseley.

It is now positively stated that Sir Garnet Wolseley is to be raised to the peerage. It is understood that this honour is to be conferred upon the General in order that he may, in the House of Lords, conduct and explain the new scheme of military reform, which he will personally supervise at the Horse Guards.

The Greek Question.

The first formal step has been taken in the renewal of negotiations at Constantinople. The Ambassadors met yesterday at the British Embassy, when the two Turkish delegates appointed to conduct the negotiations on behalf of the Porte were present. What was done, however, is not known. Probably not much. But at least a beginning has been made, and we may look to hear of some little progress. In Berlin, however, there is still doubt expressed as to the possibility of peace being maintained. Prince Bismarck is said to be convinced that it cannot; but we do not know that the authority for quoting the Prince is any of the best. In Athens also doubts are expressed as to the preservation of peace; and one report is that Turkey is trying to delay negotiations as much as possible in order to push forward the necessary warlike preparations.

The Weather.

There has been a great improvement in the weather in London. Yesterday was an exceedingly agreeable spring day. The sun, which has been so great a stranger to us recently, was visible for some time, and his beneficent influence felt. To-day is similarly spring-like and warm, and the weather has actually begun to have a settled look. It is very different, however, in Scotland. There they have had a snowfall of 70 hours' duration. Railways in nearly every district have been blocked, and even in the large towns locomotion in the streets was difficult. On the Callander and Oban line six passengers, two of them ladies, were dug out of the London mail train, having been thus imprisoned for 58 hours, suffering great privations. A party of men sent to relieve some labourers on the Highland Railway were also snowed up on Saturday, and it is feared that two of them have been lost in the drift. The hotel at Dalwhinnie, near Blairathole, is full of snow-bound passengers. The wind has also been blowing a gale, and numerous wrecks are reported along the Eastern Coast. The barque *Merlin*, of Sunderland, was dashed among the rocks near St. Andrew's, and knocked to pieces. The crew perished. They are believed to have numbered ten persons.

Terribly Destructive Earthquake.

The little island of Ischia, near Naples, was visited by an earthquake on Saturday afternoon. The shock only lasted a few seconds, but in that time the principal town on the island — much resorted to for its mineral waters — was all but destroyed. Some 300 houses were destroyed, and it is believed that probably 200 lives have been lost. Up to yesterday afternoon 102 bodies had been recovered, and it is known that many more are missing. The shock was, in the words of the *Daily News* correspondent, accompanied by a noise like subterranean thunder. Then came the crash of falling houses, mingling with the shrieks of the victims. Many were killed instantaneously, mothers being found crushed with infants still clinging to their breasts. At Villa Canetti two girls out of three playing on a doorstep were struck dead by the falling of the architrave. The third escaped as by a miracle. In Casamicciola the surviving inhabitants live in tents, fearing to trust themselves in the houses that have been spared. The earthquake was not heralded by any premonitory symptoms, and the unfortunate people had no time to attempt even to escape.

The Farmers' Alliance.

The Warwickshire Tenant Farmers' Association has been affiliated with the Farmers' Alliance. Mr. ... marked that farmers ploughed and sowed on that day, and there was no reason why they should not exhibit. The fair is accordingly to be held on the usual day.

Mr. Joseph Livesey, the father of teetotalism, attained his 87th year yesterday. Two deputations from London waited on him, and congratulations were sent him from every direction.

A child, five months old, being left in a bassinette near the kitchen fire of a house at Burnham, near Bridgwater, the clothes caught fire, and the child was so much burnt that it died soon afterwards.

Mr. John Roberts, one of the tenants on the Hawarden estate, read a paper on "The Past and Present Condition of Agriculture," at the opening meeting of the Chester Farmers' Club on Saturday.

A fire occurred on Saturday night in the Pension and Staff Office at Shrewsbury, two storeys of the building being gutted. The origin of the conflagration was supposed to have been a fire left by some painters who had been at work during the day.

It is stated that a Papal Encyclical will shortly prescribe the observance of a jubilee for Italy during the months of April, May, June, July, and August; and during October, November, and December for other countries.

DOUBLE MURDER MYSTERY

ROMANTIC FEUD

The public have lost a sensational treat through the sudden death of the man Hope, who was suspected of the murder of Mr. Enoch Drebber and of Mr. Joseph Stangerson. The details of the case will probably be never known now, though we are informed upon good authority that the crime was the result of an old-standing and romantic feud, in which love and Mormonism bore a part. It seems that both the victims belonged, in their younger days, to the Latter Day Saints, and Hope, the deceased prisoner, hails also from Salt Lake City.

If the case has had no other effect, it at least brings out in the most striking manner the efficiency of our detective police force, and will serve as a lesson to all foreigners that they will do wisely to settle their feuds at home, and not to carry them on to British soil.

It is an open secret that the credit of this smart capture belongs entirely to the well-known Scotland Yard officials, Messrs. Lestrade and Gregson. The man was apprehended, it appears, in the rooms of a certain Mr. Sherlock Holmes, who has himself, as an amateur, shown some talent in the detective line, and who, with such instructors, may hope in time to attain to some degree of their skill. It is expected that a testimonial of some sort will be presented to the two officers as a fitting recognition of their services.

On Saturday evening the Duke of Edinburgh, Prince Alexis of Russia, and Admiral Leotrine arrived at Charing-cross from the Continent, where they were met by the Duchess of Edinburgh and Prince Lobanoff, the Russian Ambassador.

The Liberal Association of Frome have adopted a resolution to be sent to Mr. Gladstone, expressing confidence in the Government, but trusting that at the earliest possible moment peace may be restored in South Africa, and especially in the Transvaal.

A woman named Elizabeth Currie, 22 years, living apart from her husband, and who was said to be greatly addicted to drinking, was found dead in bed at Liverpool on Saturday, with a bottle which had contained carbolic acid by her side.

Frances Budd, a young woman of twenty, was charged before the West Bromwich Magistrates on Saturday with abandoning her illegitimate child by leaving it at the house of a neighbour, whose son she alleged to be the father. She was cautioned and discharged, with a recommendation to apply to the Guardians.

The Bishop of the diocese having declared that the rector of Llandegfan, in Wales, was not discharging his duty to the parish, nominated a curate, who yesterday appeared on the scene when he was met by

MONEY MARKET AN...
THIS DA...

Hal...

The week opens with fresh e...
Money Market, the New York ...
the banks which had renou...
have applied for power to...
their request is likely to be co...
are unchanged at 99¼ to ⅜ fo...
½ for Account. Foreign Bon...
tinental buying, and Railways ...
better on the fine open weathe...
rities there is general buoya...
Speech and its reception throug...
regarded as favourable to busin...
movement is in Reading, Illin...
Great Western.

The reserves of the New Y...
now amount to £13,640,000, bei...
the required fourth.

The New York Exchange is u...
Call Money has fallen 1, the ra...
cent. Securities have advance...
Eries have risen ⅛ to 49¼, New...
107⅞, Philadelphia and Readi...
Union Pacific Shares 1⅛ to 123,...
¾ to 147¼, Illinois Central Sh...
Western Union Telegraph Shar...
States Bonds are ⅛ lower.

The Horse Shoe Manufacturin...
has been formed for the pu...
the patents granted to Cha...
Providence, Rhode Island, U.S...
facture for England of horse ...
with the right to take ...
other countries whatsoever, e...
States of America and Canada, a...
shoes manufactured under such p...
money is fixed at £85,000 in ca...
capital of the Company is £145,0...

Mr. Samuel Waterhouse, of ...
whose death was announced ...
according to "The Directory of ...
director of the Central Argent...
(Limited), the Central Argentin...
(Limited), the Great Northern R...
the Halifax and Huddersfield ...
pany (chairman).

The shipments of silver from ...
during the past week amounted ...
of Chester has left New York wit...

The half-yearly accounts of ...
Railway Company of Canada ...
able balance sufficient to pay ...
rate of 3 per cent. per annu...
Shares, and after carrying forw...
Detroit, Grand Haven, and Milwa...
remains £4,000 to be carried fo...
account.

The South-Eastern Railway C...
a special meeting for the 17th o...
a resolution as to the purchase o...
Hotel Company (Limited), and ...
trator to fix the purchase money.

Notice has been given to th...
debenture holders in the Old ...
that applications for fully pa...
New Flagstaff District Silver M...
five shillings each, should be ...
Wednesday next, the 9th inst., ...
the terms of Professor Vincen...
the 26th of February last, copi...
forms of application, can be obta...
citors, Messrs. Lousada and Em...
ander Kerly.

The letters of allotment and re...
Works Company of Egypt were p...

Qua...

There is now less firmness in ...
Sheffield Deferred is ⅜ down, No...
donian ⅛, and Great Eastern ⅛; ...
Brighton Deferred, and London ...
are ¼ up, and Midland an...
⅛. Amongst Foreign Bonds, Pe...
easier. Turkish of 1871 has f...
Domingo 2¼, but French Five per...
Spanish ⅛, Hungarian of 1871 and ...